Praise

Beyond The Surface Of Restorative Practices

"Marisol Rerucha unapologetically urges school districts to be unafraid of adopting and implementing holistic and healthy cultural approaches to pedagogy. *Beyond the Surface of Restorative Practices* is a social and spiritual tool, and the genius of this work is that it begins its therapeutic process with the implementers. Rerucha is mindful that educators—regardless of their racial identity—have also suffered from systemic trauma and must, too, be made whole before they can genuinely reach and help their pupils. In this current era of racial reckoning in America, this work should be required reading for all who teach or plan to enter the teaching profession."

—Nehemiah D. Frank, founder and editor in chief of *Black Wall Street Times*

"This book is right on time! An increasing number of schools across the United States are exploring restorative practices to reduce inequity in education. However, misimplementation abounds. Initiatives often fail because they adopt a narrow, "quick fix" focus on techniques (such as circles) instead of a comprehensive vision of transforming the culture. In this book, Rerucha and her colleagues provide guidance for implementing this work with integrity and in alignment with the Indigenous traditions on which restorative practices are based. Their advice is simultaneously holistic and pragmatic. Best of all, it honors sacred, ancient wisdom and traditions that respect dignity and facilitate healing, justice, and community. This is a breath of fresh air in an environment where this work is too often colonized and reduced to a bag of tricks."

—John Krownapple, educator, consultant, and coauthor of *Belonging through a Culture of Dignity*

"Marisol Rerucha masterfully weaves her personal journey with concrete strategies for implementing restorative practices in the classroom, school, or organizations of any type. This book makes a compelling case for centering trust, relationships, and community as the means for achieving transformational personal or professional growth and for building successful learning environments for both students and adults. Rerucha challenges us to join her circle and then teaches us how to use authentic and sustainable practices that build durable change in our own communities."

—Gini Pupo-Walker, state director for the Education Trust in Tennessee and school board member, Metro Nashville Public Schools

"This text goes so far beyond *what* restorative practices are and paints a beautiful picture of *why* and *how* they are to be experienced by students and adults alike. Marisol notes that 'restorative practices allow us to create a space where we can be heard, seen, and accepted.' This book creates a space for us to reflect, find healing, and walk away with a road map on how to effectively lead this life-changing work in our own circles."

—Jill Siler, EdD, superintendent of Gunter ISD and author of *Thrive Through the Five*

"*Beyond the Surfaces of Restorative Practices* is a practical guide for any school or organization that seeks to authentically build a system that honors a restorative culture. Marisol centers her work in the wisdom of Indigenous cultures and gives practitioners the necessary steps for implementation."

—Alexis Knox-Miller, director of equity and inclusion, Colorado Springs School District 11

"*Beyond the Surface of Restorative Practices* by Marisol Rerucha is a phenomenal resource for every educator. Marisol does an outstanding job of not only establishing the why of restorative practices but gives applicable strategies for how to make this a reality on your campus. The resources and examples provided throughout are tremendous. This is a book I wish that I had from my first day in the classroom."

—Beth Houf, principal and coauthor of *Lead Like a PIRATE*

"It's one thing to read a strategy. We are in no shortage of self-help books. What sets this book apart is that it's been tried and proven. That makes all the difference. This book and this author—they make all the difference. I couldn't recommend this book more highly. It's been a transformative blessing in my life, and I know that it will be in yours, too."

—Vivett Dukes, human, mother, wife, teacher, writer, advocate, activist

"This book truly goes beyond the surface of restorative practices by presenting a beautifully woven tapestry honoring the Indigenous roots of circles, the lived experiences of the authors—both personal and professional—and the necessary steps, systems, and procedures to run effective restorative circles in a variety of settings. *Beyond the Surface of Restorative Practices* is a must-read for educators seeking to run circles that can transform individual and organizational health!"

—Craig Beswick, vice president of trauma, resilient educational communities, and lifelong learning, Learn4Life

"This is an impressive and informative book that captures the importance of how restorative practices within schools can change the school's climate and culture. Every day, students enter our schools with different traumatic experiences and all they need is someone to actively listen to them. This book is filled with practical ideas for educators on how to be restorative and bring about healing. I recommend this book to all those educators wanting to be empowered with the skills, knowledge, and understanding of restorative practices in our schools and their true value for healing."

—St. Claire Adriaan, principal, Academy of the City Charter School, New York

"You must read this book if you care about meeting the comprehensive needs of students and want to create a system of equity literacy that addresses racial biases in education. Regardless of your role, this book will provide you with the transformational practices and knowledge to outline the work that we all need to do. This book unapologetically communicates that providing equity needs to move beyond something that we do and become who we are."

—John Monteleone, administrator, Lorain City Schools

"This book is efficiently structured and practical for use in a variety of settings. As I read through it, I thought of nonprofit, corporate, faith-based, and even familial applications. The lessons about culture and equity are timely, as many of us around the globe are experiencing a realization that we lack understanding of the historical trauma and lived experience of many of the people we interact with on a daily basis."

—Ginger Hitzke, president, Hitzke Development Corporation

"There is no doubt that educators, organizers, leaders, and those striving for personal growth will find Rerucha's text phenomenal. It's one thing to focus on restorative practices striving for transformative experiences in a workshop or when facilitating a meeting. It's more difficult to transfer these practices to all that we do with our students, familias, colleagues, and the staff we supervise. It's a slower burn, and it needs to be tended to consistently with care and wisdom. Rerucha inspires and consciously pushes the reader to be better, to do more, and to want to work for transformation. Rerucha gives you intense and practical advice while challenging you to do the important work of individual and collective healing."

—Tommy Valentino Ramirez, school director

"Marisol has created a genuine collection of steps for any school or organization to dig deeply in to the culture and purpose of restorative practices. This is a sensible guide for creating a true culture where all members of the community can flourish in the authenticity of their development and humanness."

—Mona Contreras, educator and counselor

Beyond the Surface of Restorative Practices

Beyond the Surface of Restorative Practices

BUILDING A CULTURE OF EQUITY, CONNECTION, AND HEALING

Marisol Quevedo Rerucha

Beyond the Surface of Restorative Practices: Building a Culture of Equity, Connection, and Healing

This book is available at special discounts when purchased in quantity for educational purposes or for use as premiums, promotions, or fundraisers. For inquiries and details, contact the publisher at books@daveburgessconsulting.com.

Published by Dave Burgess Consulting, Inc.
San Diego, CA
DaveBurgessConsulting.com

Library of Congress Control Number: 2020944734
Paperback ISBN: 978-1-951600-58-7
Ebook ISBN: 978-1-951600-59-4

Cover design by GOODSOUL
Interior design by Liz Schreiter
Editing and production by Reading List Editorial: readinglisteditorial.com

Contents

Introduction 1

Chapter one: Restorative Heartset and Mindset. 6

Chapter Two: Implementing Restorative Practices 23

Chapter Three: The Collective Agreement 31

Chapter Four: Introducing Restorative Practices to Your Community as the Organizational Leader 45

Chapter Five: Circles/Círculos: The Way to Connection and Healing. 52

Chapter six: Active Listening for Educators 72

Chapter Seven: Trauma and Resilience. 86

Chapter Eight: Responding to Challenges 99

Chapter Nine: Leadership Matters 117

Resources. 122

Glossary. 138

References 140

About the Author 144

INTRODUCTION

W e are the sum of all experiences—our own and those that we carry in our ancestral line. We are the beautiful and joyous moments as well as the mundane. We are also those moments that live in the shadows of violence, despair, heartbreak, and disappointment. These experiences form the way we see and walk in the world.

There is a proverb that states that if we stand tall it is because we stand on the shoulders of many ancestors. Dr. Sharon Grant taught me that when we join in relationships, we become a part of each other's bloodlines; this happens because we and generations after us are changed by all that we pour into each other. For this reason, I believe our ancestors include our relatives—those who share our blood—and all of those who provide us with love, support, challenge, and wisdom in this life.

And while we stand on the shoulders of our ancestors, we cannot forget to put ourselves in a position to elevate future ancestors: our children. Your future ancestors are the children in your home and in your classroom, the children who greet you as you enter your school campus, even the children who wave at you in the grocery store from the seat of a shopping cart. They are the children sitting in social service offices with their parents, in detention centers separated from their families as they await asylum, living in foster homes, and sleeping in cars or on the street wrapped in the arms of parents or siblings. We have a responsibility to our past and future ancestors to leave this world a better place than when we entered it. Once we accept our place in this circle of life, we can start to take responsibility for ourselves, our lives, and our future and become the positive change needed.

As educators, we all enter our profession with the valuable and honorable mission of taking responsibility for the learning of our world's youth. But that mission can prove to feel impossible and overwhelming when so many challenges push against us, our students, and our communities. The challenges we face in schools are as diverse as what we experience in life. Life is hard, exhilarating, boring, hopeful, beautiful, scary, blissful, and frustrating for educators and students alike.

The reality is that schoolchildren, educators charged with their learning, and district leaders are all carrying harm and trauma that has been passed down through our system and through our families. As a human species, we have a tremendous amount of work to do regarding racism, poverty, and gender equality. The way to a better world starts with each of us.

I am a forty-something-year-old Chicana, mother, and educator with an intimate understanding of human behavior and the need for healing. I mention my ethnicity and gender because these two factors have great implications in the way we perceive and interact with others. We still live in a world where our Black and Brown children are more at risk to be killed, to not graduate from high school, to live in poverty, and to be pushed into the criminal justice system. Historical trauma and systemic oppression continue to create barriers for our communities of color.

So how do we meet the needs of self, family, students, staff, and our communities with so many different and opposing requirements and desires? How do we push beyond the skin we inhabit and the formative experiences we've lived through in order to meet the needs of those who are so very different? How do we support social, emotional, physical, and academic growth? How do we create a space where students, staff, parents, and community are not just impacted positively but healed and transformed?

We do it by getting back to the ways of our ancestors. For centuries, across the world, our ancestors gathered in circles to create, problem solve, strategize, advise, and hold others accountable. We are conditioned to gather in circles, driven by our need for belonging, connection, safety, play, creativity, and communication. This way of being has come back to us in the form of restorative practices through the restorative justice movement that began in the 1970s. Restorative practices provide educators with a framework for understanding and responding to the actions of students. It also provides educators and students with the space and structure to connect with each other through reflection, listening, and dialogue. Throughout this book I will share different strategies for how to approach and implement these practices.

The honor of sharing these practices does not belong solely to me. While I continue to work with students, educators, and parents, I stepped out of the classroom in 2006, so I invited my spiritual brother, former colleague, and dear friend Pedro Terrazas, to join me by providing the lens of a classroom practitioner. He and I spent many Saturdays together over coffee talking about our work and how to best articulate this practice in words. Pedro is a restorative practices specialist who works with students, parents, and teachers in Chula Vista, California. He's also very connected to the ceremonial ways of our Indigenous ancestors and engages in this work as much more than an alternative approach to discipline. He understands that the work of restorative practices is about a deep connection to the self and others. His voice and experience will be shared alongside the work presented in these chapters in sections called Highlights from the Classroom.

Dr. Enjolie Lourdes Lafaurie and I met in Arizona when I was doing work with the Indigenous women's collective of which she is a founder. We immediately connected. What started out as a professional relationship deepened when I became her professional and personal development coach, and the relationship quickly moved into friendship and an exchange of ideas and practices. While I supported her in realizing her professional and personal goals, she supported me in connecting with my emotions. She is a phenomenal communicator who understands the importance of connection and building relationships. During one of our weekly conversations, she mentioned that she was revising her active-listening lecture, and we began a conversation that led to her contribution to this book.

Dr. Carolyn Gery is a dear friend I met in 2012 when we were both principals of charter schools who had been selected as fellows in the National Institute for Latino School Leaders (NILSL) with UnidosUS (formerly the National Council of La Raza). The NILSL experience gave us the opportunity to collaborate on national-educational-policy recommendations and to serve on panels focused on meeting the needs of Latinos and English learners. I was taken with Carolyn's vocation to research and analyze trauma and resilience.

We later worked together when I sat on the board of a large school system where she served as a chief. Her groundbreaking work there included developing early-warning systems for the high-risk student population the schools served. This allowed for a prescriptive response that culminated in an individual academic and social-emotional plan for each student that detailed the strengths of the student and leveraged those strengths to work on challenge areas. Using a social-emotional plan, a student who is able to persevere and work through multiple stressors, for example, can leverage that ability to apply to feelings of frustration when working with math. Students were then provided a network of support for integrating their social and emotional competencies with their academic competencies. Carolyn offered her lens in trauma for this book as well.

With the contributions of Pedro, Enjolie, and Carolyn, I offer this book to you from my heart, and with the best intentions for you, your family, students, staff, and all those with whom you interact. Throughout this book, we'll share terms with you that are rooted in our beliefs, derived from our culture, and used as part of restorative practices.

There are already several books and training tools explaining the methodology needed to implement restorative practices in classrooms. My intention is to offer even more—going beyond the surface of restorative practices to help you create the space for healing not only in the classroom but in your school systems, homes, and communities. I welcome and thank you for creating this space for healing and for having the courage and commitment to do this transformational work.

— CHAPTER ONE —

Restorative Heartset and Mindset

WHY WE NEED RESTORATIVE PRACTICES

In my twenty-one years as an educator, I have witnessed time and time again the power that teachers, staff, and leaders can have on educational systems and, most importantly, on students.

Human beings are social by nature, and we rely heavily on our relationships with others to form who we are in this world. We can all turn to our childhoods and recognize that who we have become is largely a result of our experiences with those who raised us (or were supposed to). When we were adolescents, our friends also had a tremendous influence on us. As adults, we continue to be shaped by our relationships with others. We learn so much from them—how to behave, communicate, and speak. Our values are based on this learning. Just as love, joy, celebration, and achievement are a part of our human experience, so are pain, loss, and fear.

We need restorative practices because of this reality. Many of us walk in this life without having healed from the pain, loss, or fear that we received in childhood, adolescence, and adulthood. Many of us also carry historical and ancestral trauma that, if unhealed, will be passed down to our future generations, causing continuous pain through a cycle of trauma. Healing and learning from our pain and trauma are possible, but only when we are willing and able to reflect on and own all of our experiences—the good, the bad, and the ugly. The truth? This is tremendously hard and scary work. But when we don't do it, we continue to keep ourselves from reaching our true potential for goodness.

Restorative practices provide a framework for being, reflecting, forgiving, and growing. We need this framework because there are so many of us who are carrying trauma that can show itself as fear, hurt, anger, disappointment, blame, distrust, control, self-aggrandizing, insecurity, and so much more. When we don't face these truths within ourselves, we continue to inflict our pain onto others.

Restorative practices are transformational in that they also offer a way of being through which systems and organizations can heal. Educational systems and those who work in them have a great deal of influence on students—on who they are and who they are becoming. Adults in school systems deserve the opportunity to grow and heal from the personal and professional harm that has occurred in their lives. By engaging and becoming truly restorative, teachers, leaders, and school staff can then offer this transformational way of being to students, parents, and their community. Imagine every person being able to communicate their remorse and acknowledge the suffering they inflicted—and ask for forgiveness and the ability to repair the damage. In order for this to happen, adults in school systems need to have the opportunity to grow and heal from the personal and professional harm that has occurred in their lives.

Public education systems carry the tremendous responsibility of providing a free basic education to all students. It is time for the United States to step up and guarantee each student a high-quality education regardless of their zip code or learning needs. The American public education system struggles to meet the needs of our Black and Brown students and has therefore created deep inequities in schools that continue in society.

Our school systems are in crisis. The struggle to ensure equity for our students becomes deeper, darker, and more difficult with each passing day. Why is equity needed? Our school systems were created to promote the ideals of white supremacy, leaving our students who are Black, Brown, Indigenous, low-income, or disabled without the access, opportunity, and sense of belonging of their white peers.

Equity is not a destination; it is a journey that includes institutional reckoning and transformation through healing. The transformation of our system can only happen when we accept the reality of why and how the system was formed and how it has harmed generations of students. Restorative practices provide a compassionate, authentic, and loving way to do this hard work.

Systemic oppression exists as a result of prejudice, discrimination, and racism fueled by microaggresions and implicit biases. This has created inequity that has resulted in academic disparities; the school-to-prison pipeline; generational poverty; and poor mental, physical, and emotional health. To focus on equity requires a transformation of the systems that created the inequity. This transformation must be centered in healing and connection and begins with resetting the foundation upon which these systems are built. The work of resetting the foundations must be collective and include the voices of all those in the community. Then the community must commit to individual, communal, and systemic healing and connection through culturally responsive and culture-sustaining practices; trauma-aware and -informed care; an intentional development of resiliency; and the embracing of restorative mindsets, heartsets, and actions. In order for this transformation to continue, the work must be consistently monitored and adjusted by the community as a whole. This is hard work, but it is so very possible. And we are all worth the work.

HIGHLIGHTS FROM THE CLASSROOM
BY PEDRO TERRAZAS

INTRODUCTION TO RESTORATIVE PRACTICES

Our ancestors have been communicating in circles through ceremony for centuries, long before restorative circles were a thing. Some of us are born into these ways; others find our way there through the various teachings of life. I was eighteen when I first found myself in a ceremonial sweat lodge.

When my uncle poured water onto the glowing stones left behind by my ancestors at the sweat lodge during my first experience with restorative circles, I felt the desire to speak or express myself. I needed release. In ceremony, elders will tell you not to speak unless spoken to and to make sure you are clear and direct with your thoughts and intentions if you're asked to say something. They tell you to focus on your prayers and ask your ancestors for guidance, clarity, and help. In that moment, I remember praying for myself and at the same time praying for forgiveness. I was carrying a lot of cargas, not only mine, but those of my ancestors. In this temazcal, I was able to express my thoughts and feelings on a deeper level than I had ever been comfortable doing before. In this círculo, I felt connected, I felt a sense of belonging, and I felt loved.

Looking back, I now realize how bound I have been to restorative practices. I started my career in education in 1998 as a substitute paraprofessional for the Sweetwater Union High School District in the city of Chula Vista, California. I then became a special education teacher and an administrator. Now I serve as a restorative practice resource educator. I've always felt a deep connection with the teaching and learning that comes from the relationships that I've built within the communities I have worked. Over the years, I began to see the people who I am in community with as relatives.

I use this term because when you reach out to someone for help or guidance or just to say "hi," you have made a relation.

I have had many experiences that required me to make significant changes in order to be the best instructional leader I can be. One change in our school district was the implementation of restorative practices during the 2016–2017 school year. The term "restorative practices" became a buzzword in the district during that school year. I was curious about what this new term meant and how we could use the practice in the classroom, so I decided to invest some time and energy into it. I attended some introductory trainings for teachers and staff, but I was still unsure about what it was and how it worked. I guess you could say I was looking for an instructional manual, a breakdown, or a how-to guide on implementing restorative practices in my daily classroom routine. Initially, I was given several resources—books, manuals, and websites—to gather information that I could use at my own site. I also attended many training sessions to help me grow with regard to this topic. There, I was inspired to learn more about restorative practices and how I could bring these teachings back to my school and embed them in the teaching community.

Restorative practices is a philosophy that promotes a healthy learning environment by building a culture of equity, emphasizing the importance of building community, and developing healthy, positive relationships while restoring relationships when harm occurs. As an educator, my goal has been to implement these practices at a pilot school in my district. It has been wonderful to lead our students, staff, and community with this initiative. I work with students, teachers, and other administrators to develop and implement what is recognized as a restorative practices model program.

One of the first things I learned was that educators have used punishments as their primary source for consequences when students misbehave. At our school, we've used out-of-school suspensions, in-school suspensions, detentions, parent conferences, and zero-tolerance policies. Trying to understand these attempts at intervention and why they are not effective is as important as any other concept about learning. Only once we've understood these interventions can we begin changing the traditional or "old school" educator mindset where control is *high* but—too often—support is *low*. Implementing a restorative philosophy in a school means using strategies that can help students in situations in and out of the classroom. One of the most important things to focus on is helping a child take responsibility when they have done something wrong, and repairing the harm that's been done.

As a restorative practitioner, it is my personal goal to walk this lifestyle in every aspect of my life, not only at work or at home but in all aspects of my daily routine. This is the beginning of how I build my system of support. I believe there is a purpose for restorative practices at every school site and that when properly implemented, it will change the culture and mindset of the whole school. The purpose of these practices is to address all harm done to children and adults on our campus and provide them with a space to heal. The healing that is produced can come in many shapes and forms.

Offering a system of support such as restorative practices on our campus has allowed victims to express any and all harm that has been done to them. Having this safe space lets them be vulnerable enough to express how they have been harmed and what they need for their healing to begin. I have witnessed this process through mediation meetings that I have facilitated. The participants have not always said "sorry" or repaired the relationship, but there has always been an agreement that all participants will respect each other mutually, as human beings. This is part of the healing that can come from having an effective RP system. Often, we feel the need for an apology to get past issues or harm that others have imposed on us. Giving an apology can be very difficult, especially if the perpetrator doesn't feel they are at fault or they owe the victim anything. Clarity with all persons involved is important here. What I've come to learn is that that clarity can come in the form of an apology but also in the form of an agreement.

WHAT DOES IT MEAN TO BE RESTORATIVE?

Let's begin by sharing what restorative practices are not: They're not new. They're not simply a step-by-step process to fix students and staff. They're not a manual full of topics to get students to share their experiences, thoughts, and emotions. They're not a training that you complete or a book that you read. They're not just about mediation or forgiveness.

Pedro and I have each been working in education for over twenty years. We understand the educator's need to see restorative practices as a framework for designing lessons or learning processes in the classroom to change student behavior. As educators, we have a tendency to try something new with a hard focus on outcomes. We want to know, "How does this work? How will this improve my classroom/teaching? When will I see a change in my students?" But restorative practices are not just an outcome.

Restorative practices are sagrados, sacred. These practices are rooted in indigeneity and offer a way of life that recognizes our responsibility for self, others, our community, our Mother Earth, and all earth's creatures. Restorative practices provide a way to both build and repair relationships with self, others, and the broader community. We adopt these teachings—this way of being—so that we can improve and build a stronger society for future generations.

Restorative practices are based on the belief that all human beings want and deserve to be heard, seen, and accepted. They are based on the belief that all human beings intrinsically want to do the right thing and embrace growth. People who have a restorative mindset and what we refer to as a *heartset* are authentic and reflective; they can build trust, listen with their hearts as well as their minds, embrace difficult and awkward situations, seek growth, and provide opportunities for others to grow. They are human-focused to their core.

Having a restorative mindset means that you have the tools and methods to guide restorative practices. It also means that you believe others are capable of wanting to address and repair harm. Having a restorative heartset means that you're emotionally grounded and you embrace vulnerability and authenticity in yourself and others.

Father Greg Boyle, founder of Homeboy Industries, a gang intervention and rehab program, believes that a truly restorative person doesn't just serve students, staff, and community, but savors life with them. He says, "We don't go to the margins to rescue but to be rescued." We recognize that we walk in life alongside students, connect beyond academic learning, and feel impact through our shared human experience. Restorative practices allow us to create a space where we can be heard, seen, and accepted. Through dialogue, we can share who we are, where we come from, what we desire, what our hopes are for ourselves, our families, and our communities. When we listen to the hearts, pain, and dreams of others, we feel truly connected in our shared experiences as human beings. We stop seeing people as the other or as having the potential to be our enemy or the bad guy. This connection is the basis for healing and problem solving.

Restorative practices are about being and doing.

In our society, we have a difficult time being direct with others about what we think or feel for fear of hurting someone else's feelings or of being perceived in a negative way. Talking with someone who you perceive as having hurt or harmed you is uncomfortable and scary. Many of us fear being judged or labeled, and we avoid real conversations. We have a tendency to shy away from conversations that may offend or make someone else uncomfortable, and instead, we live in a state of discomfort. We also have a hard time taking responsibility for our own actions that contribute to conflicts. We are not really taught how to solve conflicts or how to effectively communicate when we've been harmed. Because most of us haven't developed healthy conflict-resolution and communication skills, when conflict happens or harm occurs, many people hold their emotions in, which can result in unresolved pain that leads to pent-up anger and stress. What also happens is that we start to see the person who hurt us as a villain.

A WAY TO HEAL

We are all walking miracles with the immense power to heal. Just take a dive into researching how our bodies repair and heal themselves. Our bodies, fueled by our will, can be miraculous. When I was teaching, I would show my ninth-grade students a short video about the power of the human brain. This video showed a young girl who had half of her brain removed who had learned again how to walk, talk, and use both sides of her body. A dear friend of mine had an eighty-five-year-old grandmother who was diagnosed with terminal cancer and in hospice care. I remember receiving a call telling me that if I wanted to have one last visit with her, I needed to get in my car and make the two-and-a-half-hour drive as soon as possible. That was over eleven years ago. It is my joy to report that she lived to be ninety-six years of age. Healing is a gift. So, if our bodies have these amazing abilities, don't we also have the ability to heal our inner beings? Our minds and spirits? Of course we do.

We enter education because we believe in the future and want to make a difference in the world through our work. Working with children and youth provides us the opportunity to have an influence on their development as thinkers, feelers, and the future of our world. We care deeply about our students and our work. The reality is that many of our students enter our schools dealing with the impact of trauma. Trauma exists. We must offer healing. Who better to embrace the opportunity for healing than educators?

In some households, sharing and reflecting on emotions is not part of the family culture. My home was full of love, but there was always something to be done, and emotions were almost a luxury of time that no one could afford. My parents were divorced, and they were both open with my brother and me but only to a certain point. We could ask questions about sex, and the effects of drugs, cigarettes, and alcohol. We could even talk about depression—but only as it related to other people. What we couldn't do—as kids or adults—was ask about their divorce or try to discuss any ways that their actions may have harmed us. My parents either weren't willing or able to go into that space. At some point in my adult life, I realized that I was being held captive by pain from my childhood, which resulted in anger, disappointment, and depression.

I became a mother at nineteen years old. Pretty early on in my adulthood, I decided I wanted to have a healthy relationship with my parents, just as I wanted with my own children. I needed to figure out how to heal from events that happened in my childhood. A gift of realization was bestowed upon me in the process of acceptance and forgiveness. For every choice we make, there is a consequence. I realized that those who hurt me through their words and actions were really acting from their own pain, which had nothing to do with me. In turn, I saw the way my pain caused me to harm others. It was essential that I end this cycle. I made the decision to embrace healing.

As mentioned, restorative practices allow for individual and community healing. Actually, I believe this to be generational work that can transform familial and collective futures. I use the acronym HEAL to describe my foundational beliefs when providing restorative practices training because the training centers on:

HUMANS. We are all human beings living the same human experience. We deserve respect and love and interpersonal communication, regardless of differences, such as age, sex, ethnicity, and any other forms that our differences take. We have a responsibility to ourselves and each other to understand and acknowledge that we are whole beings with intellectual, emotional, spiritual, and social needs. Restorative practices are both a holistic- and human-centered mindset and heartset that put relationships of self and relationships with others at the forefront. This acceptance of self and other is a way of healing that allows us to walk in this world authentically.

EMPATHY. We are more alike than not, regardless of any noticeable differences. By listening with our hearts, with dignity and respect, we open ourselves up to the experiences of others. We can then begin to see patterns of experience and frequency. Most of us at some point have been targeted for the way we look. Through this, we begin to notice that factors like (but not limited to) poverty, race, abilities, and body size can increase the frequency of negative experiences. When we share our experiences with one another, we begin to connect and build bridges of understanding. This leads to accepting the need for equity and inclusion in our work, schools, and communities.

AGREEMENTS. By having agreements that are reviewed and revised regularly, we continuously remind participants that their privacy will be honored (unless someone is abusing them or they are considering serious harm to themselves). This creates a culture of trust that allows individuals and communities to be authentic and vulnerable, leading to reflection and potential healing of emotions and harm. It also allows for the true celebration of joy and love. Agreements should include how you will treat one another, celebrate one another with joy, work out disagreements or harm done, and engage in healing as a community.

LOVE FOR SELF AND OTHERS. This is what allows us to heal. As long as we are alive, we have the ability to grow and learn. We embrace a growth mindset because we are committed to being the best humans possible. Growth is difficult and uncomfortable. In order to grow, we have to brave discomfort within ourselves and between others. We grow through our experiences and interactions with others. In this work we must encourage, recognize, and celebrate love, joy, and success.

RESTORATIVE PRACTICES START
WITH THE SELF

My friend Ginger shared a statement with me from an episode of *Oprah's Lifeclass* made by Iyanla Vanzant that changed my life: "It's self-full to be first, to be as good as possible to you. To take care of you, to keep you whole and healthy. That doesn't mean you disregard everything and everyone. But you want to come with your cup full. You know: 'My cup runneth over.' What comes out of the cup is for y'all. What's in the cup is mine. But I've got to keep my cup full." Of course, I've heard and thought I understood the analogies of self-care that described filling our own cups or putting our masks on first in an airplane in case of losing cabin pressure. But I had it wrong. I thought the ultimate goal was to fill my cup so that I could empty it again. It never dawned on me that I was to keep my cup full for myself and allow it to overflow so that then I can give that extra goodness to others. This learning came to me when I was almost broken.

Parenting has been the greatest gift and most difficult challenge of my life. I have a deep and profound love for my daughters, whom I credit for all that I am. At nineteen years old, I gave birth to Camerina (Mina), and Emilia (Mimi) was born when I was twenty-one. I wanted to give my girls so much—not just material things but a continual demonstration, through my example, of their value as human beings. I had to exit the toxic and harmful relationship with their biological father, and he willingly left without turning back when Mimi was a mere three months old. During those early years, my best friend, Atiya, whom I consider my sister, helped me raise my daughters. Imagine being in your early twenties and being ready and willing to change your life to help raise your sister's kids. Everything that Atiya and I owned (it wasn't much) was ours together, and it was reserved for providing for the girls. The four of us, and our families, have been blessed by our relationship. Because of her partnership, and with the support of my family, I was able to graduate from college, earn my teaching credential, and start my career in education.

During my first year teaching, I met Daniel. He is a beautiful being who has a profound respect for himself and who soon saw me as his life partner. After we married, he spoke to the girls about adopting them and since they agreed, he began the process. Their biological father showed up at the courthouse and signed away his rights to the girls. Within a month, Daniel was signing his name to make them his children. With the signatures of their biological and adoptive fathers, Mina and Mimi were given away and then immediately claimed. At the adoption hearing, I remember the judge shaking Daniel's hand and telling him, "This is a really good thing you're doing." At that time, the girls were nine and ten years old. They had known Daniel since they were four and five. About a year and a half after the hearing, we had Sophia, our third daughter. Daniel asked me, the girls, and our family not to let our youngest know that her sisters were not Daniel's biological children until she was old enough. He didn't want her to ever feel that they were different from her or that they meant less to him. My girls have an amazing father who has loved them with all his being, provided for them, played with them, guided them, and most importantly, continually prayed for them. They have a mother who does the same.

Our girls are now in their mid-twenties. They are good human beings who are smart, funny, talented, and beautiful. But they struggle and have done so for many years. Even all the love, guidance, support, and experiences their tribe tried to provide couldn't overcome the harm caused by abandonment, which impacted their self-worth. Separate incidents of harm have occurred between us, and there is no clear path to restoration. As I write this, I feel a pain that burns tears in my eyes. I can't love them enough or change the outcomes of their lives. I have to allow them to continue making choices that may lead to more harm in their lives.

I realized that I had engaged in unhealthy patterns of behavior that came to light when I was diagnosed with high blood pressure and anxiety. I had to release my daughters to live their lives, and I had to embrace their choices and subsequent outcomes. By holding on and trying to control and guide them, I was making myself sick. And I couldn't do that anymore.

Here is why the metaphor about putting the mask on yourself first before putting it on a loved one who needs help is misleading. It only considers self-care during a time when there is an extreme, life-threatening emergency. I have no idea how many times I've been on an airplane; not once, thank God, has there been a need for those masks to drop. The reality is that we need to engage in showing compassion for ourselves every single day so that we can healthfully take care of others.

Keeping my cup full is a new practice for me, one that requires actions that come from a deeply personal and reflective place. I keep my cup full by being patient with myself and being aware of my thoughts, physical sensations in my body, and my emotions. Meditation and prayer allow me the time and space to do these internal investigations about what my needs are. Here are some of the things I do to try and keep my cup full:

- Connect with Daniel in some way every day.
- Talk/text with Atiya at least once a day.
- Do something to help my body feel healthy, stretched, and strong (a total work in progress).
- Practice daily prayer and meditation.
- Visit my therapist regularly and more frequently as needed.
- Eat breakfast.
- Drink a lot of water.
- Take medication and supplements as prescribed by my doctor.
- Sleep at least seven hours a night.
- Connect with my girls via text or in person as often as possible.
- Check in with my mom, dad, aunt, and brothers.
- See, or check in on, my dear friends regularly.
- When a stressful situation occurs, check in with myself, and make a decision on how to react and what to say (or not) that represents who I am.
- Visit my chiropractor, acupuncturist, and/or massage therapist regularly.
- Engage in community prayer.

By doing the above regularly, I am filling my cup so that I can walk in this world ready to support and give to others, including my family, staff, and strangers. There are other things I need that also fill my soul and inspire me. I am someone who needs to engage with beauty and movement regularly. For this reason, I need to dance, read, write, travel, visit art museums, and engage in creative thinking and activity. This practice of keeping my cup full has allowed me to respond to life's challenges and blessings in a healthy way.

FORGIVENESS

"IF YOU WANT TO FLY, YOU GOT TO GIVE UP THE SHIT THAT WEIGHS YOU DOWN."

—Toni Morrison

Forgiveness allows you to release yourself from being controlled or led by the pain of another. We have all been hurt, harmed, or maybe even destroyed by another person's actions or words. Those of us who get through the pain do so with the gift of true forgiveness. When someone intentionally hurts you, it can be soul crushing. Being harmed has made me doubt my worth and made me feel ashamed. Forgiveness is essential for those who want to live happy lives. But here's the catch: to forgive, you have to be willing to accept that you have been hurt, feel that pain, and be willing to release the way that holding on to the harm has served you. This is such a difficult process that in *Rising Strong*, Brené Brown equates it with the actual process of grieving the loss of someone you love. She writes, "Forgiveness is so difficult because it involves death and grief." In forgiveness we have to be willing to let our hurt, blame, and victimhood die.

I learned at an early age that forgiveness isn't about the other person. It's about me not allowing my anger, hurt, pain, and disappointment to define who I am. As hard as it can be to forgive someone who hurt me, it's even harder to forgive someone who has hurt my loved ones. The hardest thing has been learning to forgive myself. It took over twenty years for me to fully forgive my daughters' biological father. The easiest part was forgiving him for any pain he caused me. I was in my early twenties and a practicing Catholic at the time. I remember talking to Father Brown, our parish priest, telling him that I didn't want to carry the weight of being angry or hating my daughters' biological father for abandoning our family. From my perspective, I had so much to do—finish school, take care of my girls, and be the best person I could for myself and for them—and I didn't want to carry the burden of the pain. I remember asking Father Brown, "How do I forgive someone who isn't around and who isn't asking for forgiveness?" Our conversation taught me that forgiveness is for me.

Sometimes, especially when my daughters are struggling in life, my resolve to maintain this forgiveness is tested. As my daughters grew, their pain, especially that of my eldest, stoked intense anger and resentment toward their biological father from me. There was a moment during this process, over twenty years after he left, when I realized that by not forgiving the impact of his actions on my daughters, I was holding on to him. I realized that not forgiving him actually served me. As long as I held on to the pain and trauma he caused my daughters, I could blame him for their struggles and challenges. By finally releasing him, I then had to see my daughters' responsibilities in their life choices. I also had to acknowledge that while I did the best I could, I also bore responsibility for some of their pain.

Forgiveness of myself has been the hardest: forgiving myself for the choices I've made, for the ways that I have hurt others, for allowing myself to be hurt. A key to taking care of myself has been reflecting and owning the hurt and pain I've caused myself and others. This has allowed me to embrace the process of forgiving myself.

Restorative practices provide a process for harm to be examined from all perspectives. This examination opens a pathway to forgiveness that releases us from the chains and weight of harm.

ADDITIONAL CONSIDERATIONS

When Pedro and I do the work of restorative practices, we've found that the following concepts should be acknowledged. They aren't conditions that *need* to exist for restorative practices to be successful in your classroom, school, or district, but they are the solid foundation upon which *our* collective and individual way of being is built:

- Our ancestors are those who lived before us and have now passed into the next life. Their actions and connections to us, each other, the earth, and all elements continues to live through us and ceremony. We are guided and protected by them.
- We are all relatives, regardless of shared blood. As human beings, we are related and we honor, accept, and recognize each other as family.
- We are future ancestors; our children are future ancestors. We have responsibilities as future ancestors to create goodness in our lives and to care for each other.
- We are connected to Mother Earth and all its animals. We have a responsibility to protect and care for both.
- We are constantly watching out for ourselves and our families. We strive for balance in our lives, taking care of our needs and those of our partners and children before we attempt to take care of others.

In order to do the work, we must have a solid foundation within ourselves, our families, our homes, and our organizations. In the next chapter, we will explore how to build a foundation of trust and collective action.

— CHAPTER TWO —

Implementing Restorative Practices

THE ONE THING YOU CAN'T TAKE AWAY FROM ME IS THE WAY I CHOOSE TO RESPOND TO WHAT YOU DO TO ME. THE LAST OF ONE'S FREEDOMS IS TO CHOOSE ONE'S ATTITUDE IN ANY GIVEN CIRCUMSTANCE.

—Viktor E. Frankl,
Man's Search for Meaning

I have witnessed the miracle of healing and connection that can happen to individuals, teams, and community through the framework of restorative practices. It is hard work. But it's possible.

I joined education because I wanted my life's work to have an impact on the future of our communities. As a teacher, I was student-focused and protective of our youth. I had zero tolerance of anyone speaking badly about our students or their abilities. I was a fierce mama bear who was ready to attack when confronted with adults who spewed harsh, punitive beliefs and perspectives toward students and their families. It was my long-held belief that schools should be safe places for students, filled with support, guidance, and protection. As teachers, we were charged with the moral obligation to believe the best existed in each student who crossed our doorways—even when they didn't believe in themselves. And especially when generational pain prohibited their parents and families from believing in them.

When I transitioned into administration, I maintained my focus on students, but over time I developed a profound respect for my role in supporting, guiding, and protecting staff, too. It was my friend and mentor Shelley Burgess who guided me into this understanding. As educational leaders, we have a moral obligation to extend our deep beliefs about student ability to that of our staff and colleagues. Once I understood this, I was able to witness the transformation that happens when staff are part of collective decision-making and responsible for acting on agreements.

Six years of my career were spent in a local elementary school district, where I served as a site administrator. The three years I spent as an assistant principal provided me with an intimate and thorough understanding of behavior and special education. It was as a principal that I first experienced the magic that happens when you truly trust staff and provide space for their voices in identifying areas of need and in creating action plans. My staff and I dove headfirst into a structure called Positive Behavioral Interventions and Supports (PBIS), and by employing this program, we quickly became a model school for our district. This framework includes the specific teaching of behavioral expectations reinforced by feedback, reteaching, and extrinsic recognition and rewards.

My time in the elementary system taught me that we are all, regardless of age, human beings looking for connection and wanting to be seen and heard. It was during this time that I learned:

- Behind our actions, there's a purpose and function for our behavior.
- Recognition of efforts is an effective way to support change for students and adults.
- Interventions work when implemented consistently.

- Systems can change when you provide space for staff to have voice and ownership and when site administrators facilitate and guide change while holding all accountable for agreements made.

My introduction to restorative practices began in 2012 when I became the principal of an alternative charter high school and started working with the dean of students, Tommy Valentino Ramirez. At that time, Tommy was implementing restorative justice in place of the punitive-based disciplinary process used in most traditional schools. At the school, he held circles regularly within his leadership class of students and as a regular part of staff meetings. Tommy explained how in an incident of harm there is the "victim," the person who was harmed, and the "aggressor," the person who caused the harm. He described how restorative justice allowed for the victim to clearly express the harm that was caused to them and how the person who caused the harm then had the opportunity to absorb how their actions affected others. There was then a chance for the person who caused the harm to take responsibility for the damage caused and take measures to repair what they had damaged or broken.

In 2015, I joined a large system that had made a commitment to restorative practices. There, I met a coordinator, Cynthia Burton, who had convinced the leadership to allow her to train all staff, students, and willing parents in the restorative practices model. During the two-day training, we learned the philosophy behind the practice and engaged in check-ins and circles. At the charter school, we used these practices with students but never implemented them deeply and consistently with staff.

During this training, I witnessed the need for adults in our system to reflect and connect with themselves and each other. In my most recent role as a district administrator, I've been able to witness what happens when restorative practices are implemented with staff. Restorative practices have allowed my team to create and maintain a space for us to engage in honest, brave reflection, leading to individual and collective healing. Restorative practices transform the lives of everyone, not just students and families.

As I mentioned earlier, I firmly believe that educators enter the field because we have positive beliefs about the future. We want to make a difference in the world by working with children and youth, which provides us with the opportunity to have an influence on their intellectual and social-emotional development. I have found that educators are compassionate and have a lot of love for students and the community. If we are so driven by all these positive motivations, love, and compassion, then why do we struggle with student behavior? Why do we struggle with the behavior of colleagues? Why do educational leaders have such a hard time addressing adult behavior? As is true with so many things, the answers to our struggles lie within us.

Far too often, in too many schools, teachers, staff, and administrators are frustrated with student behavior. There is always a lot of blame to go around . . . blaming parents, blaming previous teachers or other schools, and blaming the students. Frustration comes from student behavior that looks and acts like disrespect, lack of focus, disengagement, limited effort, bullying, inattention, and impatience. It's natural and human for educators to feel disheartened, frustrated, and even hopeless when it comes to working with challenging behaviors.

Alive in this frustration and despair is a structure that places teachers in an elevated position as the givers and keepers of knowledge, exposure, and opportunity. This position comes at a cost and sacrifice. Teachers have a minimum of five years of university study. Most spend countless hours before school, after school, on weekends, and during vacation preparing for their students' learning and classroom experiences. In this structure, students are the receivers of the beautiful gifts that educators are trained and have sacrificed to give.

If you are taking the behavior of others as a personal attack, that is a sign that you are struggling with your ego. The ego can keep us stuck in a space where we care too much about what others think about us. This can look like us being hurt and stuck because we don't understand why others don't like us or support our work. It can take the form of our getting very angry when we think someone has disrespected us—or comparing ourselves, our classrooms, or our work with the success or failure of others. The ego acts within us through competition. I have found some great resources that have helped me understand, become aware of, and make the shift away from ego. My greatest teachers have been heartbreak and pain . . . they have released me from my ego. They have taught me that I have no control over anything but myself and my reactions to what occurs. If you're looking for resources to learn more about ego, look up Eckhart Tolle's books or his conversations with Oprah Winfrey on her *SuperSoul Sunday* show or podcast.

Restorative practices are based on a belief in humanity. This way of being is about authentic connection and community. When we see ourselves in each other, our response to challenging behavior is more caring and compassionate. So how do you go about establishing these connections and building this community?

Educational leaders must do this work with their staff. "Healthy relationships between and among all members of the learning community—including students, teachers, administrators, staff, parents and caregivers, and the local community—are essential for effective learning" (Gregory and Evans 2020, 8). As much as teachers and other school staff need to connect and see the humanity of their students and the families of their students, they need to see and feel the same for one another. This happens when they're

IN LAK'ECH

As part of my introduction to restorative practices, I use an excerpt from the poem "Pensamiento Serpentino" by Chicano playwright, author, director, and founder of El Teatro Campesino, Luis Valdez because it represents the deep connection and responsibility we have to be our best for ourselves and others. It describes *In Lak'ech*, the Mayan concept of oneness between humans, animals, and all the elements (earth, air, water, fire).

provided with frequent opportunities for personal and shared reflection that is guided by mutual agreements and protocols based on the concept of circles.

Before we jump in, I just want to thank you, on behalf of my ancestors, myself, and my future ancestors for answering the call to this work. By learning and walking this way, you are opening yourself to growth and healing. By sharing this way, you are providing your community with the chance to heal and grow as well. This way of being with self and in community transforms individuals, relationships, families, and society. If you're ever nervous or worried about this work, please know that there are people throughout our world doing restorative practices with the same hopes as you.

Restorative practices are part of Restorative Justice in Education (RJE) initiatives and build community and connection through reflection and sharing of experiences and their attached emotions. Restorative practices have Indigenous roots that include council work. It's through councils that community is built, decisions are made, individuals seek advice, problems are solved, and harm is repaired. There are many groups that gather to engage in council work. During a training on council work provided by Circles for Change and the Ojai Foundation, our trainer, Yamin Chehin, would repeat, "This work is not therapy but it can be therapeutic." This is true of council work and of restorative practices, as we have the opportunity to reflect and heal.

Restorative practices is a philosophy that emphasizes the importance of building community and developing healthy, positive relationships while restoring relationships when harm has occurred. Restorative practices have been a way of being and communicating since our ancestors first built communities. We are fortunate that many people have kept this way of communication and of solving issues and conflict. It is in our blood. Around the world, in all ancient civilizations, you will find reverence for the practice of the circles, a vital part of restorative practices.

Current research and teachings on restorative practices say that these practices are founded in the restorative justice movement of the 1970s. In restorative justice, there is a mediation between victim and offender. The goal of the mediation is to provide victims with the opportunity to explain how the incident of harm impacted them, their loved ones, and their community. The offenders can take this chance to reflect on the effect of their actions and take steps to repairing harm. Restorative justice acknowledges that harm can't be erased, but it can be repaired. This work continues to be used throughout the world as part of justice reform efforts.

Restorative practices includes active listening and observation, team building, and circles of dialogue. It is always trauma-informed, and considers data, both pre-implementation and ongoing through the practice. Any work with restorative practices should start with the creation and refining of agreements and foundational statements for organizations.

HIGHLIGHTS FROM THE CLASSROOM

BY PEDRO TERRAZAS

MY FIRST HANDS-ON EXPERIENCE WITH RESTORATIVE PRACTICES

During the first year of my teaching job, I was introduced to a program at my middle school called MIP (male involvement program). My principal asked me if I would cofacilitate this program on campus with someone from a local agency. This was a program adopted from a community-based organization and implemented at our school to help deter young male at-risk students from gang affiliation, substance abuse, and unprotected sex. Little did I know that this program would reconnect me with my reason for becoming an educator. It was missing the most important element that ignites any reaction, the sazón to any recipe that an abuelita puts her hands on. The program came with a cofacilitator, a curriculum, and an expected outcome, but it didn't have one thing: corazón.

Our program would meet once a week in my classroom during lunch, and it was such a good feeling to see my boys walk into the room with their heads held up high. They knew they were the desmadrosos of the school, and they wore the label with pride, but they also knew they had been chosen for a special program. Unfortunately, this pride of being desmadrosos came from years of the school system failing to connect with them. While they struggled academically, they were able to gain attention through their behavior. They also knew that they had just entered a safe space, a place where they had taken an oath to not be judgmental and to always agree on resolving any conflict.

It was here in this young men's group where I began to heal my own cargas. I saw an opportunity to do something good for these young men. I saw an opportunity to make all the wrong things I did as a youngster right. In this space I began to forgive a person who had inflicted a tremendous amount of hurt in my life and had broken my spirit with one sentence, an event that would eventually lead me down a self-destructive path in my education. It created insecurities I never thought I had.

It's important to acknowledge when we've been hurt or have hurt others. We're not always able to recognize either situation, but when we accept what has happened to us or what we have done to others, then, and only then, are we able to forgive—ultimately allowing us to heal. In this program initially created for my "at-risk" students, I was able to accept that I too was misunderstood as a young man, and because of that, I reacted as a misguided youth and said things that would hurt others, ultimately hurting myself.

It was because of this program that I was able to have empathy for these young men and for myself. The healing that took place in MIP gave me a feeling that I hadn't encountered in my previous years in education. Restorative practices help a victim forgive another person for the harm inflicted upon them. It doesn't mean the victim will ever forget the experience, but it will give them a new opportunity to heal and move forward with their relationships.

— CHAPTER THREE —

The Collective Agreement

Through professional learning communities, work groups, or committees, your organization can continue providing staff and community the power and space to take ownership over the collective work it does.

It is a true honor to be selected to lead one of these groups. With experience, training, and practice, I've come to believe in the power the alignment of an organization's mission and vision can bring to the everyday work. That power and magic is the result of guiding members of a team and coming to an agreement on what our mission, vision, and beliefs are. These statements become the North Star for all decisions, and everyone has a voice regarding the direction of the collective work.

Systems and structure are a part of all aspects of our lives. My experience has taught me that, in partnership with a committed and courageous community, any work is possible with these two things in place. Every group, school, system, and organization that hopes to have an impact while honoring its members needs to have a strong foundation guiding their work and their strategic and organizational plans. This foundation includes the collaborative development of four different statements describing the group's agreements, beliefs, mission, and vision. Every organization has a mission and vision statement. Most have belief statements and some type of agreements, which can be in the form of norms or a code of conduct describing how individuals will treat one another and how they will act as a group.

These foundational statements should be developed with input from all members, then reviewed at the start of each meeting and reviewed or revised annually. Most systems already have these statements developed. More often than not they are created, placed on a poster and on important documents, then forgotten about. When these documents are read only at a board meeting, they aren't central to the work.

Collectively, these foundational statements set the tone for your organization's culture, where the restorative mindset and heartset lives. Having these collectively created statements helps during difficult and challenging times. They act like anchors to ground discussion and decisions. In this chapter, you will be provided with a way to guide your community through the development or revision of your agreements, beliefs, mission, and vision.

COLLECTIVE DECISION-MAKING

When working with groups and making decisions, it's important that everyone have the opportunity to express their agreement or disagreement throughout the process. This takes time and can be frustrating when you feel that you may be working against the clock. However, this work and time is well spent. People feel valued when their voices and input are taken into account.

In meetings, it's important to explain your process and make sure everyone understands what certain signals mean. You can do a practice run on the process using the signals described below.

THUMBS UP, THUMBS SIDEWAYS, THUMBS DOWN

One simple way of expressing agreement or disagreement, which works well with small groups, is to have people use their thumbs or a finger. Thumb/finger up signifies agreement. Thumb down means no agreement, and the person then needs to share why they don't agree. A thumb sideways means that they will support and follow the agreement, although they aren't totally excited about it. As a group, you continue to revise the decision until everyone either has their thumbs up or sideways.

GREEN, YELLOW, AND RED CARDS

This strategy is especially effective for large groups. You will need green, yellow, and red index cards for each person that are large enough to be seen across the room you are working in. A green card held up signifies agreement. A yellow card signifies a question or can mean the same as a sideways thumb: unenthusiastic agreement. A red card signifies disagreement. If there are yellow cards, any questions need to be posed and answered, or the holders need to be acknowledged as in agreement. If there are red cards, the disagreement needs to be voiced and the decision is revised until everyone agrees either enthusiastically or unenthusiastically.

HOW TO HANDLE HOLDUPS

At some point when crafting a decision such as an agreement, you will have people who get really caught up on the wording. If this becomes an issue, there are a few things you can do. You can invoke facilitator/guide rights and state that you are going to use particular words and explain why. Or you can review word choices to make sure that the important components of the decision or agreement are included. Then you can ask for permission to be a wordsmith, or even ask for volunteers to sit with you at a different time to work on the phrasing. I have found that this saves time and gets the process moving. Make sure to build in time, through a break or a working lunch, to finalize the wording, whether on your own or with a group (you can select volunteers and ask them to join you or leave the invite open). Once you've worked out the wording, bring it back to the whole group to vote on.

SHARED RESPONSIBILITY

We cannot lead or do this work on our own. I have found that most members of our community want to help and support an organization's process. For this reason, I developed a number of roles that I ask members to take on. You can add to these roles, change the titles, or redefine them as fits your style and organization. If you're working with a small group, you can ask for one volunteer for each role, or if you're working with a large group, these roles can be divided among table groups that can be set up however you like. It's important for participants in my trainings to have free choice in their seating.

Let your team know that you are going to need help through this process and are going to offer roles that they can volunteer to fill. Post and review each role and description.

TIME GUARDIAN. Must take note of time given to complete tasks and keep the group informed of time remaining. The time guardian is responsible for giving a two- or five-minute warning before breaks and calling the group back together.

CRITICAL FRIEND. Assessing the proceedings. Did we meet our stated goals? What is still needed or what can be changed? The critical friend is responsible for collecting data and providing feedback when the day's activities are complete.

MOTIVATOR. Responsible for providing genuine, detailed, and positive feedback to each member of the group. The motivator can decide if they'd like to give feedback verbally or in writing.

COLLABORATOR. Must come up with ideas for process and lead the group in committing to one, whether it's using thumbs up, cards, or other techniques. The collaborator is responsible for guiding group decision-making.

TEAM BUILDER. Responsible for two short team-building activities (five to ten minutes each), including a summary discussion of the activity.

WARRIOR OF THE PEN. Responsible for documenting all decisions made and reminding group members (through email, phone, or text) of commitments made for action and follow-up.

AGREEMENTS

At the start of each workshop or training, the group I'm working with creates a set of agreements that guide what we expect of ourselves and each other. Agreements are also known as norms, codes, rules, or even accords. I like to use the term "agreements," though I sometimes lean toward using the term "understandings." Agreements are the code of collective action that state how the group will be working together, communicating, and establishing a framework from which to address conflict and make decisions. These agreements are created collectively, and they should be reviewed at the start of each meeting and addressed when appropriate. Agreements define the way an organization or group has agreed to work together. They help establish and reinforce expectations of engagements.

THE BASICS OF AGREEMENTS

- Agreements are expectations of behavior.
- A common set of agreements supports your team in working together effectively, holding each other accountable, and solving problems when issues arise.
- Agreements provide clarity regarding communication.
- Agreements can be revised as needed and should be reviewed at the start of each meeting.

PROCESS FOR ESTABLISHING AGREEMENTS

The time needed to create these agreements will depend on your facilitation. In general, this work takes me an hour and a half.

ESTABLISH. Organize participants into tables or small groups of ten people or less. Select and explain the decision-making process and explain the basics of agreements.

ASK. Have everyone think about and write down the most important expectation of behavior they have when working with others. Ask them to be clear and specific. For example, "be respectful" is too vague. More specific examples could include: start and end on time; trust that others have the same positive intent as you do; communicate any question, doubt, or incident of perceived harm within X amount of time. Once everyone has written the agreement that is most important to them, have them share with their group.

CHOOSE. Ask groups to collectively create or select the one most important agreement. It should be specific, clear, and written from a positive—not punitive—perspective. Let groups know that they are sharing the one agreement that is the most important and not adding them all together and trying to pass them off as one. When that happens, it communicates distrust in the process and distrust that the collective as a whole is capable of proposing sensible agreements.

SHARE. Have all the tables share their agreements. Clarify the agreements so that they are clear, concise, and make sense. If a table has an agreement similar to one that has already been crafted, ask if the existing one is acceptable, or revise. You do not need to end up with any particular number of agreements. Some agreements can be combined. What's important is that you have

36

the agreements this particular group has voiced and taken part in creating.

VOTE. Once you have the final set of agreements, take a vote on them. These are the agreements that will be used for your time together. If you are doing this work with your staff, let them know that these are the agreements for this school year.

REVISING AGREEMENTS

Once you have your established agreements, they should be posted and reviewed at the start of each gathering. They should also be reviewed and revised annually.

REVIEW. Assemble your organization into groups and put one of the following prompts forward: How have agreements been beneficial to our work together? What needs to change or be added to our agreements to make them more effective?

SHARE. Provide time for individuals to share their responses with their table groups. Each group must come up with a summary of what needs to change or be added. Have groups share and write down their recommendations on a white board, poster paper, or a computer screen.

COLLABORATE. Using the comments provided by each table, begin the process of reviewing the current agreements as a group, making any revisions and polishing phrasing together.

DECIDE TOGETHER. Vote on changes and additions one by one, finalizing agreements for the next school year.

BELIEF STATEMENTS

Belief statements describe the heart of the group/team/organization and explain what it values most. These statements are created collectively and should be reviewed annually to be validated or revised. Like agreements, there is no magic number of belief statements that your organization or group should have. What's important is that everyone has a voice in creating them and agreeing to the final versions.

Belief statements clearly describe your collective beliefs about the world, driving the mission and vision of your organization.

> SEE THE RESOURCES CHAPTER FOR
> EXAMPLES OF BELIEF STATEMENTS.

PROCESS FOR IDENTIFYING VALUES AND CREATING BELIEF STATEMENTS

EXPLAIN. Discuss the purpose of belief statements and provide examples.

REVIEW. Have group members reflect on the values your organization promotes and that center the purpose for the work. Values are the foundation upon which your organization is formed, guiding its action.

GENERATE IDEAS. At table groups, have people discuss and come up with a list of what they believe are the core values of your organization.

> SEE THE RESOURCES CHAPTER FOR
> EXAMPLES OF CORE VALUES.

SHARE. Ask tables to share the values they came up with. If there are values that are similar, decide as a group which is most appropriate.

DISCUSS. Once you produce a list, have an open discussion about these values.

DIVIDE. Assign a value to each table. If there are more values than tables, you can divide people into more groups so that only one group of people has to work with one value.

ASK. Have each individual write a statement addressing these questions:

a) What do you believe about life/society/humanity that promotes you to action/work?

b) What are the foundational beliefs behind the need for the value assigned to your table? For example, if you have social justice as a value, you might say that social justice needs to be promoted because injustice exists. If teamwork is a value, then you could discuss the importance of collective action.

c) After each individual has had a chance to reflect and write their statement, they will share with their table.

DECIDE. The table will then create a table statement by discussing and voting on each individual's statement.

a) As a whole group, begin the process of reviewing each table's belief statement, making any revisions necessary and voting on changes and additions one by one.

b) Finalize the belief statements for the next school year and vote.

SEE THE RESOURCES CHAPTER FOR AN
EXAMPLE OF A VALUE STATEMENT.

> ### HOW MANY VALUES?
>
> The goal is not to reach a certain number, but to have a list of values that your group feels are the most important. The number of values is totally up to the team. I prefer to keep the number on the smaller side because it allows you to focus on what is most important. What's critical is that the group decides on the values together.

MISSION AND VISION STATEMENTS

Every organization in existence probably already has a mission and a vision statement. Mission statements describe the organization's purpose for existing. They state the overall goal and tell how you do the work and for whom you do it. Vision statements state what you want to achieve as objectives that guide internal decision-making. These objectives are measurable and tangible.

Most mission and vision statements are stagnant. While these documents are foundational, they should also be timely and relevant to the current work of the organization. An organization is like an organism: it is alive and changes. Their foundational documents should be flexible and align with shifts in the organization, so it's important to refresh, review, and revise mission and vision statements with input from all stakeholders.

This process will entail reflection, writing, and sharing. During the reflection and writing time, I love to play music. I try to keep it at a volume that can be heard but not be distracting. I also ask for permission. For some people, it can be very hard to concentrate with music playing. If it bothers anyone, then I just ask for silence. While they write and reflect, I act as the timekeeper, using the timer on my phone.

ASK. Start by asking everyone to write about, reflect on, and discuss the most important aspects of your organization's mission with the following prompts:

- What do you love about this organization?

- What has been challenging about the work?
- What do you want to communicate during our time together about yourself?
- What do you want to communicate during our time together about your organization?
- How do you want to communicate during our time together?
- How do you not want to communicate?

REFLECT. Guide your team through the reflective exercise around their capacity to truly engage in your organization. This must be done without judgment.

Provide group members with paper and ask each of them to draw a heart while thinking about all that they appreciate about the work of their organization and those they impact through that work. This is not a competition about who has the biggest heart for the work—the size of the hearts they draw might reach the edges of the paper, or it could float in the middle or on the side—but a reflective exercise.

Now ask them to think about all the responsibilities they carry and all the things they focus their attention and time on. Once they have this established in their hearts and minds, ask them to think honestly about the capacity they have to do the organization's work while drawing a second heart inside to show that capacity in relation, more or less, to their heart for the work. Whether they have the two hearts rubbing right against each other or their capacity hearts are one-eighth the size of their heart for the work, what matters here is that everyone is honest with themselves.

SHARE. Now that everyone has a list of answers and their hearts, ask them to take turns sharing. If you have a large group, then this sharing will happen in table groups. Everyone should share their answer to one of the prompts above and their heart drawing.

FILL IN THE SPACES. Once all have shared, have everyone go back to their hearts. Ask them to fill in the space between the small and the big heart with words or visuals that represent gentle, loving kindness and nonviolence toward self and others.

REVIEW. Read the current mission statement aloud. You can either have hard copies of the statement for them to work with or you can have them write it down.

DISCUSS. Have everyone get with a partner and discuss the following:

1. What do you like? What is missing?
2. What do we do?
3. How do we do it? For whom?
4. What value do we bring?
5. What is your fight?

REVISE. After this discussion, partners can either approve of the mission statement as is or they can make revisions. Provide time for this. Partners will share their work either with the group or table (depending on the number of people). As a group, a decision will be made to either approve the current mission statement or engage in revising.

SEE THE RESOURCES CHAPTER FOR SOME EXAMPLES OF MISSION STATEMENTS.

VISION STATEMENTS

In my work, I have seen vision statements that are very short and simply describe the ultimate desired outcome of an organization's work, such as: "Historically oppressed and marginalized individuals and communities are healed and transformed." Other vision statements include the tangible actions the organization is willing to take to meet the mission and vision.

SEE THE RESOURCES CHAPTER FOR AN EXAMPLE OF A VISION STATEMENT.

CREATING A SAFE AND BRAVE SPACE FOR RESTORATIVE PRACTICES

By engaging in collective review, revision, and/or development of foundational statements, leaders create an environment of trust. Through the process, you are communicating that everyone has a voice that is valued and important to your organization's work. With this trust established, you can open a space for honest communication and vulnerability, which open the door to deeper connection. Restorative practices and the work of building connection and community require honesty and vulnerability to prevent and repair harm and restore relationships.

HIGHLIGHTS FROM THE CLASSROOM
BY PEDRO TERRAZAS

In the 2018–2019 semester, our site joined four other restorative practices pilot schools, making our high school and feeder middle school the fifth and sixth schools in our district to adopt the restorative practices model. Our district department of Equity, Culture, and Support Services has proposed a framework for the pilot schools that emphasizes the importance of building community and developing healthy, positive relationships.

At my school, the intention is to strengthen an already-existing positive school culture by building relationships with the student body, staff members, and community. It also involves restoring relationships when harm occurs. We have a culture-and-climate committee that creates and proposes exercises and allows staff to express their insecurities about teaching or any other questions about restorative practices.

In my role, I've found it's essential that I meet regularly with the administration team. Two core understandings in my work are: (1) that everyone is different, as is their healing process, depending on what healing they want for their lives; and (2) that if the district is moving toward restorative practices, these ideas and philosophies should be implemented by all stakeholders.

— CHAPTER FOUR —

INTRODUCING RESTORATIVE PRACTICES TO YOUR COMMUNITY AS THE ORGANIZATIONAL LEADER

O nce you've led your organization through the development and/or revision of foundational statements, you will have set the tone for the introduction and implementation of restorative practices. By creating these foundational statements with stakeholders, you have established a culture of trust where your community will be willing to enter the safe and brave space necessary for the work of restorative practices.

As a leader in your organization, you can now introduce restorative practices to your system. If you are part of a larger system, like a school, you can do this work with your team or with your classroom. If you are an organizational leader, such as a principal, superintendent, or school board member, and you are serious about working in this way, it's critical that you become restorative and practice this way of being.

Many leaders approach this with a train-the-trainer mentality and send representatives or task someone to specialize in this work. When it is done, the people sent to training are considered the experts, which creates the sense that this work and way of being belong to them alone.

Some systems that try to implement restorative practices err by not truly immersing all members in this learning and way of being. You can deepen your learning by attending training or hiring a consultant or trainer, but the best way to deepen this work is to commit to the practice. Start this way of being at home. Apply the tools of reflection, dialogue, and listening with your heart and mind. This work isn't just a process; it's a way of being that supports you in meeting your purpose in work and in life.

Once you know that you are willing to fully embrace a restorative heartset and mindset, it's time to introduce restorative practices to your system.

> **MODIFY**
>
> Please know that the following processes can be used as is or in a modified form with students of all grade levels.

PREPARE

Reach out to people in your organization and also embrace online platforms that can connect you to practitioners throughout the world. Find a partner who is also introducing this work or who is already deeply practicing it.

Because part of what restorative practices do is offer help to those in need, have community resources readily available to staff and students. Resources should include access to mental health services, emergency shelter, food, and other resources. Have information available with a confidential staff member or in a place that students and staff can access it quickly and discreetly. Provide online resources as well as locations for in-person services, and have employee assistance program (EAP) resources available for staff. Ensure that your staff receive mandated reporter training.

You can also provide notebooks or tech tools for participants to confidentially keep track of their notes and written reflections.

Prepare resources and references for team members to enrich and extend their learning. Resources include: a copy of this book, articles, research, and online resources. Prepare the following training in a format that can be shared with staff so that they can in turn use this with their teams and students.

Inform the people in your organization that you are going to be deepening your connection with one another as a community through restorative practices. Let them know that this work may be uncomfortable but that you will continue building a culture where all feel safe and brave. Also let them know that this work takes time.

> **PREPARE AND SHARE**
>
> Trainings can be made available in a format that can be shared with staff so that they can in turn use it with their teams and students.

STARTING THE PRACTICE

PREPARE. Select which collective decision-making strategy you're going to use as a group. Frequently check to see whether others are ready to move on by voting. Remind your staff and students that all school staff are mandated reporters and if a student is being abused or thinking of seriously harming themselves, it must be reported to ensure their safety.

INTRODUCE. Share what restorative practices are and why you are bringing this work into your school culture.

REVIEW. Review your organization's agreements, values, beliefs, mission, and vision. How are restorative practices aligned with these foundational statements?

ASK. Have everyone take out a notebook and let them know they'll have a few minutes to think about and answer three different questions. (You will need to work out the timing based on the overall schedule you have, but I've found that two to four minutes is generally enough for participants to reflect and write.)

Set an alarm and read the first question, then reveal the subsequent question after the alarm sounds and repeat for the third question. These three questions are:

What do you know and/or believe about restorative practices?

What do you want to learn and know about restorative practices?

What is working and not working at your school regarding behavior and school culture?

> SEE THE RESOURCES CHAPTER FOR MORE PROMPTS
> FOR WORKING WITH STUDENT OR FAMILY GROUPS.

THE BASICS OF RESTORATIVE PRACTICES

It is a way of being that can and will change your organizational culture. This is accomplished with:

- Frequent communication that allows us to see each other's humanity through check-ins, circles, and mediation;
- Authentic sharing of experiences that may require vulnerability;
- Active listening and observing;
- Opportunities to reflect, heal, prevent, and repair harm;
- An understanding of trauma.

Team building is critical to this work because through reflective— and even fun—activities, it builds community, connection, and trust.

SHARE. Provide additional time for participants to share with a partner or small group. Then ask for responses and write them on a large sticky pad or white board.

Share the data of your school culture. This should include: disciplinary referrals/suspensions/expulsions; attendance (student and staff); staff retention; and any other data that your local area may collect, such as the Healthy Kids Survey in California.

Share that you will be implementing/strengthening restorative practices, explaining its basics and history in restorative justice.

CHECK-IN AND CHECK-OUT

The easiest way to integrate and begin the practice of connection is to implement check-ins and check-outs at the beginning and end of any meeting. This can be done before small group work with students, at parent meetings, during any type of staff meetings, and really any time that you gather with members of your community. The check-in allows everyone time to share, listen, and get to know one another. At the start of any meeting or gathering, you can let everyone know your system is restorative and that connection with one another is critical to your work together. Have a check-in and check-out questions and review agreement.

SHARE. Let everyone know that the goal of a check-in is to take time before engaging in work together to get to know each other and set a tone of community. Discuss agreements that are critical to the development and maintenance of community. Be flexible, but always remember that we are mandated reporters. State that we must take action to protect students if anyone is being hurt or considering hurting themselves.

INTRODUCE A TALKING PIECE. Explain that only the person holding the talking piece has the floor to speak. It's their time to share and everyone else's time to listen. Everyone else should refrain from speaking. This can be hard since we are so used to connecting verbally. During check-in, we connect by listening and allowing the words of others to resonate within us.

CHOOSING A TALKING PIECE

A talking piece can be anything participants bring in that has meaning to them or anything that they are willing to have others use in this exercise. It can be something you bring with you, ask someone else to bring, or happen to have handy. For example, I bring a small wooden figurine of three women that my aunt brought to me from a trip to South Africa. I see the three women as my daughters. I also use a rock in the shape of a heart that my sister gave to me as a reminder of the love that she has for me. The talking pieces can sit in the center of the circle. Each speaker can use the talking piece used by the previous speaker or exchange it for another piece in the center. Make sure this is done only during their time.

BEGIN. Review the process and ask for a volunteer to start. Hand over the talking piece and then proceed with checking in, going to the left of the person who starts and asking a question like one of the following:

- How are you feeling today?
- What was the high or low point of your evening/weekend?
- What is something you are looking forward to today or this week?
- What was the biggest challenge in completing a recent task?
- What are you proud of this week?
- Are you more energetic in the morning, afternoon, or evening?
- What is something that surprises others about you?
- Describe a typical evening at home after school or work.

WHY LEFT?

We go to the left because our hearts are in the center of our chests, in between our lungs, but slightly tilted to the left. It is through the left side of the heart that blood flows and sustains us.

- Who are you and why are you here?
- What's your favorite song/band/music genre and why?
- Tell us your name and three things you love to do without explanation. (This works great if you are short on time or there are a lot of people.)

CHECK. Once everyone has shared, make sure they're ready to start the meeting.

CHECK-OUT

To close each meeting, it's important to do a check-out. The agreements and process for check-outs is similar to that for check-ins, but the kinds of questions you use should be different. Here are some samples:

- What was your favorite thing about today's meeting?
- After our time together, what are you looking forward to?
- Who did you appreciate in the circle and why?
- Could you reflect on our time together and make a statement starting with, "I heard . . ."?
- What are some changes you need/want to make after our time together?

If time is short, check-out can be quick. Try asking members to share briefly in response to a prompt.

SEE THE RESOURCES CHAPTER FOR SOME SAMPLE PROMPTS TO USE IN CHECK-OUTS.

Checking in and checking out are great ways to learn about each other and identify any potential needs. This should not be a chore. If time is short, you can use the quick-round suggestions or either check-in or check-out, as opposed to doing both. There are no hard or fast rules here. What matters is that you are connecting with each other.

CHAPTER FIVE

Circles/Círculos: The Way to Connection and Healing

Our educational systems and organizations are hierarchical structures. School administrators and teachers have authority and power over others. Individuals in these roles determine how they assert this authority and power. For your system to implement restorative practices, your leadership must be willing to approach staff and students as equals in humanity—in circles.

ONE TEAM'S JOURNEY

What works in classrooms can also work well with staff. Why? Because we are all human beings who want to be valued and engaged in our work. When I held my first staff meeting with my last team, I sent them an agenda that outlined expected outcomes of our time together, and I set the expectation that each member of our team would be responsible for one or more aspects of our meeting. Each of the roles described earlier (time guardian, critical friend, motivator, etc.) can be shared by more than one person if there are more people than assigned roles.

I was surprised by how excited my new staff members were to embrace these roles. Time and again, I've learned how much staff feel valued when space is created for them to actively participate and have a say in the vision of our work and the steps to make our collective goals a reality.

Our system was very fortunate to have a parent-involvement coordinator who embraced restorative practices. She attended a training for restorative practices and then convinced the leadership at the time that our parents, students, and entire staff should be trained. About a year after I arrived, all our staff were trained using the International Institute for Restorative Practices model. My staff and I then had a common framework with which to engage in the practice.

I have been honored to witness the miracle of healing that the protocols and processes of restorative practices can have in the workplace. In every job I've ever had, there has been some type of conflict that existed between members of teams, organizations, and schools. With each change of school or system, as an educational leader, I became more adept at building community with the staff and students and leading to a transformative culture. The most magical experience came from the most difficult of circumstances I had ever encountered.

I joined a team that had been working together for years. My predecessor had built the position and department I came into as the leader. A few people had previously moved in and out of the team, but when I arrived, there was an existing core of seven (three men and four women) who were consistent, and with the addition of a new male member, there were four men and four women total, not counting myself. They looked pretty typical for a group of educators in our area. The original core were three white men and four Latina women spanning in age from their early twenties to mid-fifties. They had been working together for many years, and when I joined them, I had the opportunity to see and experience their interactions and culture from an outside perspective. This group, with the addition of a Black male who was hired after my arrival, provided direct services to students that resulted in those students making drastic changes to their lives. These services, and each staff member's mentorship, provided students with an alternative to the lives they knew. The staff was individually and collectively responsible for guiding students who were changing, and even saving, their lives. As with any group that has been together for a long time, they were like a family. Like most families, they shared years of joyful memories along with years of harm, baked-in layers that never had a chance to heal.

I walked into a common type of familial dysfunction. In this work family, there were two distinctive sides, three males and two females, with the other members floating in between. As the newest member and the new "boss," both sides sniffed me out. They would come to me with passive comments about others or would ask to speak to me one-on-one about issues. Eventually, I would hear as many as eight different perspectives about the same issue. In short, each side didn't trust the motivation of those on the other side. Both sides truly felt like they were the most committed to our collective work and to our students. Both sides also acknowledged that the other side cared about students and could do really good work, but they had a sense of distrust in the others' motivations, made accusations of controlling behavior, and doubted their commitment to the collective work.

Restorative practices were mandatory training for all members of our school system. This training set the stage for us to engage in the work of circles/círculos and connection with colleagues and students. We all attended and engaged in the training, and we began the practice of check-ins and check-outs—though it was infrequent. As a team, we had already established our agreements, mission, vision, beliefs, and decision-making processes. At some point, it became clear that we needed more.

I met with our restorative practices trainer, Cynthia Burton, to discuss and plan a circle/círculo that would open up connection and communication among everyone on the team. I sent out an email with an agenda and said we would be discussing our team and expectations, addressing historical issues that had been brought to my attention, and finding a way to work together. During that meeting we reviewed and added to our agreed-upon norms:

- Respect the talking piece.
- Speak and listen with respect.
- Speak and listen from the heart.
- Remain in the circles.
- Honor privacy.
- Use "I" statements.
- Put away and silence your phone.

We then started with our first round of sharing. I asked everyone to share a happy memory. This served to start each of us off in a good space with happiness in our hearts and on our minds. Then I provided the prompt for the second round. I asked, "How do you feel about how we work as a team?" Once we all shared, I moved out of the circle and to the board, where I had written on a large notepad, "What's working and not working with our team?" As every member shared, I took notes. We moved to the next page of the notepad, where I wrote, "How have you been affected, hurt, or harmed by the way we work as a team?" This was solemn work. All members were honest and listened to one another attentively.

I then broke them up into pairs and asked them to engage in a listening activity that took them through the process of dealing with harm. Once we came back to our circle, I gave the team time to write and then share their answers to these questions:

- Are there changes you need to make?
- How is this going to impact the team?
- How do we hold each other accountable?

During the check-out, I asked for feedback on the process. I also offered to meet with anyone who wanted to brave a mediation to address any harm that they had either caused or experienced. During the following weeks, I facilitated mediations between multiple members of the team. Some of the issues discussed were years old but merely boiled down to misunderstandings and miscommunication. Each mediation ended with all participants feeling heard, seen, understood, appreciated, and relieved. This work was amazing, and I was honored and proud to be part of a team with such open and courageous people.

We had a miraculous few months, with monthly meetings that included a whole-group circle/círculo as well as check-in and check-out. Almost immediately our team shifted from a lack of trust to a sense of belonging and community. We began working together as a team, and connecting with one another in a more authentic way. I noticed fewer conversations happening on the outskirts of our team and more happening inside of it.

Then, slowly we became more busy with new-program implementation, another physical move, the implementation of a grant-funded program, and training. We were focused on the work and dropped the circle/círculo time. I took our newly established team connectivity for granted. I didn't realize that our team remained fragile and a great divide would reopen between the two plates of our continent. The two sides collided and caused an eruption that almost destroyed our team.

Ultimately, two people carried the burden of this clash and engaged in a verbal confrontation that almost destroyed our team and could have ended one or both of their careers in our system. These two team members were alone in the office and had a disagreement that—on the surface—was about moving furniture. Their interaction erupted into what was described as a shouting match that resulted in angry tears, accusations of harassment, and a report to the central office. What we had built was almost destroyed in the blink of an eye, and the team quickly divided into two sides again, with each side protecting itself. I didn't know what to do. But I knew that the community we built had been real, and I trusted that there was a possibility we could have that again.

I spoke to each of the two individuals separately to allow space for their side to be heard and provide some feedback. At our next team meeting, we addressed the issue as a group. Things were so tense and fractured that I had no idea if we could ever mend. I told the team that if we were not able to reconnect as a work family, that at a minimum, we needed to figure out how to work together with honor and respect so that we could get through our workdays and continue to meet our students' needs. We spent three hours in that room. One of the first people to share was a younger staff member who expressed that she felt like she was being forced to pick a team. She said, "I am team 'us.' There's not a men's team or a women's team; it's just our team.'" After she spoke, each person in the room made the commitment to listen to one another and sit in the discomfort of awkward silence. We also resigned ourselves to being okay if there was no resolution once our time was done. During this meeting, every single team member was brutally honest about their feelings and experiences. For the first time, there was sharing of childhood trauma by one participant and deep insecurities about work from another. There was an ownership and understanding of sensitivities that led to reactions and responses. Things were shared that brought light to sensitivities. We discussed relationships. Those of us who had been married for a long time talked about the impact our marriages have on the way we learn from and respond to others. There were long stretches of dark silence that felt like broken glass. Finally, someone would speak up and collect the silence and then transform it to sound like hope. By the end of our time together, both parties that had the blowup not only apologized to each other but held each other and truly saw the other for the first time.

HIGHLIGHTS FROM THE CLASSROOM
BY PEDRO TERRAZAS

It's important not to see this as a step-by-step process that needs to be followed like a tight regimen but rather as part of a practice that flows naturally based on the needs of your students.

At the high school where I work, the process is one that allows many opportunities for healing. A student can be referred to restorative practices by our leadership team, counselors, teachers, and support staff. The intent is to find a common space of reconciliation, peace, and harmony. These are not your typical outcomes, but they are very important to acknowledge when trying to resolve problems that occur in the classroom.

EXPLAINING THE PROCESS

A student who is referred to restorative practices acknowledges the program is in lieu of suspension, and that student is given the opportunity to understand the value of staying in school as opposed to being sent home or kept in detention. Upon entering our restorative room, students are met by the facilitator and assigned a space to work. The initial communication can vary; many times, students feel like this opportunity is punitive and therefore still a punishment. There are other interventions at schools that focus on restoring relationships that can create a feeling of skepticism. Skepticism exists when our mindset is more focused on punitive consequences than a process that provides a space for reconciliation and healing. So it's very important to explain what the process will be like at the first opportunity to connect with students as they make their way into restorative practices intervention. Simply understanding why they have been assigned and what we, as the restorative team, hope to accomplish brings a calmness and reassurance to any individual that enters the room. Once we establish an understanding of mutual respect and communication, we can begin the program.

CLASSROOM STRUCTURE

Really effective classroom environments provide multiple opportunities for student engagement through reflective thinking, reading, writing, listening, and talking about learning with connections made between self, content, others, and community. I set up my classroom environment very intentionally to promote not only engagement and reflection but ownership of the learning. One of the first things that I provide is space for dialogue, as this facilitates the beginning of community in my classroom.

I put students into groups after reviewing the purpose of the day's learning and expected outcomes and ensuring all students understand the protocol. Each member of the group has an explicit role that they select. We use the normal roles of team facilitator, notetaker, timekeeper, and reporter. Empowering your students with this type of involvement can help overcome issues with sharing, class participation, engagement, and self-confidence. Once group work is complete, each reporter is responsible for sharing the group's work/discussion with the class. This structure is a great foundation on which to build circles/círculos.

I challenge you to create your own model that accommodates the learning environment where you teach when you begin implementing restorative practices in your classrooms. The work of restorative practices in the classroom can take many different shapes and forms. Organizing your classroom into a circle is not the only way for it to be restorative. Restorative practices are more than a thing that you do; they're a way of being. Your classroom environment should be built on a foundation of love, joy, trust, respect, and a willingness to grow individually and together.

FORMATION OF CIRCLES/CÍRCULOS

Leonardo da Vinci's *Vitruvian Man*, from around 1490, depicts human proportions using a man in two superimposed positions and inscribed in a circle and square. The image reminds us that we are physiological, whole beings represented geometrically by circles. This affirms for me that at any time, regardless of the number of people present, circles are the perfect form for us to meet in.

In a restorative culture, there is a regular time for specific groups to engage in reflective dialogue that goes beyond check-ins and check-outs. The goal of circle/círculo time is to provide structure for the practice of reflection, healing, accountability, and growth. The circle is critical to the development and maintenance of community, as it provides community discussion, sharing, and connecting, and it can be used for content discussion as well. In the circle/círculo, underlying issues can be brought to the surface, thus offering an opportunity for healing of any harm that has occurred and the prevention of harm or serious conflict.

For any type of group, you can offer a regular circle/círculo time. Think about how powerful having a consistent circle/círculo in your school system would be for your classroom, staff, school board, C-level staff, leadership, parents, community, school site council, grade level teams, content area teams, or professional learning communities. By providing this time for staff, your system ensures that they are able to facilitate and support student healing and academic, behavioral, and social-emotional growth.

SETTING THE CIRCLE/CÍRCULO. You can set up the physical circle/círculo any way that you want, but I suggest finding or creating a large space where a circle can be made with chairs. You can also have participants stand or even sit on the floor. There should be no desks or tables in between participants. After letting participants know that you will be moving into a large, sharing circle/círculo, identify the space being used and move furniture as needed.

I recommend creating a center in the middle of the circle/círculo on the floor that can hold talking pieces or any other items of importance to the group or related to the discussion. A mat, cloth, or round item can be used as the center.

Have everyone bring a chair, stand behind it, and arrange the seats in a circle using the center as a guide. I like to bring in an extra chair that no one sits in and place it in the circle in between two participants. This seat represents anyone who may be absent and also those people who are not present in the room but who are present with us—our parents, our friends, our spouses and partners, our ancestors. Once everyone feels well spaced, have them take a seat.

The following is a protocol that you can use in your circle/círculo:

AGREEMENTS. Create or review agreements for the circle. Ask participants if there are any agreements that they want to add. As the facilitator, it's important that you reinforce agreements immediately and with a soft, yet firm, tone.

INTRODUCE THE TALKING PIECE. If you have participants bring in a talking piece, the first quick round can be used to share about it. You can decide if you want to use your own talking piece or have participants bring theirs each time you meet. Have them introduce their piece and explain why it's important to them, then have them place it in the center.

ADDRESS THE EMPTY CHAIR. If you choose to have an empty chair in the circle/círculo, ask the group why they think there is an empty chair. In my explanation, the chair represents anyone who is physically not with us. We hold the chair open for them, as they are a part of our group. Before we begin, I hold a few moments for us to name anyone who is represented by the chair. During sharing, you can either skip the chair or you can leave the talking piece on the chair for a few moments and sit in silence to bring forth the presence of the people who aren't present but who you honor.

SET THE FLOW. Choose the flow of the talking piece and explain the protocol to circle/círculo participants.

The talking piece ensures that the person who has it is given the time to share. If a member wants to pass, they hold the piece during their turn, say "pass," and move the talking piece to the next person. If you have more than one talking piece in the center of the circle, you can have members switch pieces when it's their turn to respond to the prompt. There are several different ways of circulating the talking piece. I always start by sharing the prompt and asking for a volunteer.

- To the Left: After the first speaker, we move the talking piece to the person on the left. I ask the group why we go to the left. Most people answer, "Because that's the side where our heart is."
- Freestyle: With the talking piece in the center, participants decide when they are ready to share. Set the expectation that everyone participates; they can still "pass" but must get up from their seat, go to the center, pick up the talking piece, and say "pass." The first person goes to the center, picks up the talking piece, returns to their seat, and shares. When they are done, they get up, return the piece, and sit down. Once they are seated, the floor is open for whoever wishes to go next.
- Called to Share: The first speaker calls on the next person to share. They must get up from their chair to hand the next person the talking piece. That person can keep the talking piece or select a new one. Continue calling on one another to share until everyone has had a turn. Remind everyone

that the facilitator is also a member of the group and can be called to share or go last once everyone has spoken.

SEE THE RESOURCES CHAPTER FOR SAMPLE
PROMPTS FOR YOUR CIRCLE/CÍRCULO.

AGREEMENT. Once everyone has shared, repeat the agreements.

BASIC AGREEMENTS FOR CIRCLES/CÍRCULOS

Before engaging in this work, it is important to establish a set of agreements for the time that you are sharing.

- Respect the talking piece. Only the person with the piece speaks.
- Speak and listen actively from the heart with dignity and respect.
- Use "I" statements.
- Remain in the circles.
- Honor privacy. Don't discuss what is said in the circle with others (but note that if someone is hurting you or you're hurting yourself, then we will get the needed help/support).

There are lots of ways to use the circle/círculo format to explore different issues. I'm very traditional in my practice and like to keep everyone in the whole group setting or with partners. I've experienced really powerful circles/círculos that take on different formats, and I plan on using them as I continue working with organizations.

FISHBOWL

A fishbowl circle/círculo is a way to promote insight and strengthen the bonds between and within groups. In a fishbowl circle/círculo, the group is divided in two. One group will be on the inside of the circle facing in, and the rest of the group will observe from outside the circle. During the fishbowl, only the inside group speaks and responds to the prompt. The outside group is provided the opportunity to observe and listen before sharing themselves later. This format can be really helpful to build bridges between community groups.

Groups can be split any way that fills the need of the community. Some group pairing examples are:

- teacher/student
- parent/student
- parent/teacher
- classified staff / certificated staff
- administration/staff
- administration/student
- parent/administration
- one grade level/another grade level

The inside group will position themselves around the center area and use a talking piece when it is their turn to speak.

Once the inside circle is done, the outside group takes turns sharing about what they learned from the inside group. It can help for the facilitator to provide sentence starters.

SEE THE RESOURCES CHAPTER FOR
SAMPLE SENTENCE STARTERS.

As you become more comfortable with the practice, you can try new ways of building the circle/círculos experience for your community. Always critical is the implementation of the agreements.

THE PROCESS FOR MEDIATION

Mediation is a way to repair harm between people. All participants need to be willing to engage in this process, which must be facilitated by someone who is trusted by all parties. During mediation, it's important to be real at all times. Due to high emotions, the mediation facilitator should remain calm and, regardless of what is said or done, not react with anything but firmness and love.

PROTOCOL FOR MEDIATION

If possible, meet with each party separately before bringing them together. This will give you the opportunity to plan for the mediation. If this is not an option, bring the parties together in the same room. Position yourself in a space that allows you to protect both parties and yourself, if needed.

ESTABLISH GRATITUDE. Thank each participant for being brave and willing to engage in mediation to discuss and repair any harm that occurred. Let the participants know that you will ensure their emotional and physical safety. Thank them for their trust, then review agreements for your time together. You can either use general agreements established in school, or if possible, you can establish agreements directly with the participants.

EXPLAIN. Review the goal of mediation and explain the process:

- You will be facilitating and guiding the dialogue through questions and clarification.
- Everyone will have a chance to share what happened from their perspective.
- If someone hears something they think is untrue, ask that person to trust you and accept they will have a chance to share once the speaker is done.

Introduce a talking piece, if necessary and appropriate. Begin by saying something like, "My goal today is to help you (and the other/s) sort out what happened so that it doesn't happen again."

SEE THE RESOURCES CHAPTER FOR QUESTIONS
TO USE WHEN INITIATING MEDIATION.

LISTEN. If a student is upset, they might raise their voice or become physically agitated. Since they are upset, let them explain. If they use curse words, don't interrupt and reprimand them. Let them explain and release the emotion. Listen to them. If you really listen with your heart open, you will be able to connect with their emotions and see their perspective.

After each person shares, ask clarifying questions, summarize, mirror back responses, affirm (but don't agree or disagree with) the emotions that are present.

> SEE THE RESOURCES SECTION FOR
> EXAMPLES OF AFFIRMATIONS.

NEXT STEPS. It's important for the parties involved to have the opportunity to acknowledge and own their roles in the harm that was caused. Guide the parties to determine next steps. If there is action needed to repair harm, then you will need to guide them through this. If forgiveness is something that any party is seeking, facilitate with questions:

- "What are you seeking forgiveness for?"
- "How will you ensure that you won't engage in the behavior that caused harm?"
- "Are you able and willing to forgive?"

REVIEW. Summarize the mediation, including any agreements or acts of restoration that are planned. Set a date and time to follow up. Close the mediation with a check-out: "What's one word that describes how you're feeling after the mediation?" Check in with all parties shortly after mediation to see how they are doing.

STEP FORWARD

This activity has been used in social justice and equity work for decades. The purpose is for participants to reflect on others, themselves, and humanity. I often choose to use this activity on the first day of training. It opens the door for people to be vulnerable in a safe space.

LINE UP. Create or find a space where participants can line up shoulder to shoulder, facing in the same direction.

ESTABLISH QUIET. Explain to the participants that this is a silent activity. Let them know that some people may laugh and some may tear up—all emotions are okay here, but it is important that we honor each person's experience and maintain a commitment to not talking.

ASK. Read a prompt and ask the participants to step forward, turn around, and face the line if the prompt applies to them. Repeat the prompt.

> SEE THE RESOURCES SECTION FOR SAMPLE
> PROMPTS TO USE WITH THIS ACTIVITY.

STEP FORWARD. Instruct the participants facing the line to look at and acknowledge those standing with them. After they do, ask them to rejoin the line.

ASK AGAIN. When everyone is back in place, read the next prompt.

FORM A CIRCLE/CÍRCULO. Once everyone has had an opportunity to share, thank them for their participation and for sharing their thoughts with the group. Form a circle/círculo with everyone while standing to debrief.

Review some simple agreements:

- You will all listen to what is being said by one speaker at a time without interrupting.
- You will not comment on what others share.
- You will allow their experience to be their own.
- You will share your experience.

ONE WORD. Conduct a one-word round using a talking piece. Each participant will say one word that describes how they felt either during or after the step forward exercise. Participants will have another chance to speak, so make sure they stick to one word. Pass the talking piece until everyone has shared their one word.

DEBRIEF. For the next round, pose this question: "How does this activity help us learn about ourselves and others?" Remind participants to use "I" statements and to speak from their experience. They are not to talk about what any specific person shared about themselves when stepping forward.

Have participants reflect and write about the following prompts:

- Describe the activity you engaged in today.
- Why is it important to be different from others and to find commonalities with others?
- What did you learn about yourself and others?

SYSTEMIC FOCUS ON INDIVIDUAL STUDENT PROGRESS

At the alternative charter school where I served as principal, the staff had been trained in conducting circles/círculos, but they did not occur regularly within each classroom. Large circles/círculos were held when there were issues in the community and in Associated Student Body

(ASB), which was facilitated by Tommy Valentino Ramirez. We also held check-ins any time we held staff meetings to ask how the staff were feeling.

Starting before my tenure, the staff gathered once a week for what they referred to as their student study team (SST). This was not the SST of a traditional system, which leads to potential special education assessments. During this hour-long meeting, a team sat in a circle around a large table to discuss issues happening with students and teachers and came up with ideas to support the students. There was no real system to document the issues, assign a staff member, or track interventions, celebrations, and referrals.

As the new principal, I stopped the meeting and brought to light the lack of structure. I asked for input, and the team created a system using Google Docs and Google Sheets. After that, three times a week, the staff had a set time to meet, discuss, and track student needs, interventions, and successes. Twice a week, the entire staff (teachers, administrators, office staff) met in the computer lab to review and add to a spreadsheet that held information regarding each student. They followed up with each other in person and met with students. Once a week, a team would meet to review updates, provide feedback to teachers and staff, identify interventions, make referrals, and assign staff members to work with particular students. The team consisted of the principal, the dean of students, an academic counselor, a special education resource specialist, an attendance/assessment coordinator, a safety/facilities supervisor, a school psychologist, and an administrative assistant.

My role as the school principal was to ensure that time was allotted for this work and to provide feedback and encouragement to the staff. The system worked because it provided each member of the staff time to reflect on and document connections with students and—primarily— because it was created by staff for staff.

> ## TOOLS FOR MAINTAINING A RESTORATIVE CULTURE
>
> - Clearly identified and agreed-upon beliefs and expectations of the restorative culture your system is committing to.
> - Ongoing training for all staff and students in restorative practices, including orientation for all new staff.
> - A data-collection system to monitor the qualitative and quantitative impact of restorative practices. Quantitative data collected should include referral, suspension, and expulsion rates. Qualitative data can be collected through surveys and the recording of stories from students, staff, and parents.
> - A clear system for mediating and repairing harm. This can include adult and peer-led mediation. The co-creation of ways to repair harm is something that will take members some time to get used to, as most are more accustomed to being told what the consequences for harm should be in documents that address violations of local education and penal codes.
> - A dedicated and consistent time for students and staff to engage in dialogue in circles/círculos where the community and individuals can reflect on hopes, goals, trauma, and issues impacting students, the school, or community.

ACTIVE LISTENING

Think back to the story of my team at the beginning of this chapter. What made it possible for us to come back from the edge? First, everyone was able to recognize the humanity of the other. There were also some key things that every team member agreed on: each member was focused on and had the ability to connect with their students; they embraced growth and wanted to improve; each of them was brave, authentic, and willing to speak their truth. Crucially, each person listened.

HIGHLIGHTS FROM THE CLASSROOM
BY PEDRO TERRAZAS

RESPONDING TO HARM

When students arrive in the restorative practices interventions room, the intake process involves them filling out a form that asks five questions. We ask students to answer these questions in brief sentences, leaving an opportunity for the facilitator to expand on the answers later:

1. What happened?
2. What were you thinking at the time?
3. What have you thought about since then?
4. Who has been affected by what you've done—and in what way?
5. What do you think you need to do to make things right?

These questions are important to relationship building and are part of the foundation of restorative practices. Too often students, in other processes, are simply "dealt with." When they come into an administrator's office, they're asked what they have done but not given the opportunity to explain why they made the choices they did or what triggered the behavior. Most importantly, they are often not given the chance to explain how they're feeling. So, in our process, students are given the opportunity to explain themselves through these intake questions, and they're given a chance to express the reasoning behind their actions. As facilitators, we begin building relationships in this moment by asking key questions that give us an understanding of how an individual is feeling emotionally and physically. This period of communication is very important because it provides our students with an opportunity to address harms and make amends. During this time, we develop a better understanding of the harm inflicted (if any) and the student develops empathy for both the harmed individual and the self.

— CHAPTER SIX —

Active Listening for Educators

BY
Enjolie Lourdes Lafaurie, PhD, CHt

A s a psychologist and educator at the community college level, I find that students can sometimes struggle to integrate the inherent individual focus in psychology with the needs of groups within society. The emphasis on personal responsibility and mastery of oneself can be difficult to reconcile with the experiences of marginalized groups. According to the Substance Abuse and Mental Health Services Administration, those from the LGBTQIA community experience a greater propensity to suffer from mental health issues despite their resilience and vast gifts in other areas (Medley et al. 2016). Viewed on an individual level, the locus of the problem can seem to reside within the person. If the rejection and marginalization experienced by the LGBTQIA community is accounted for, then responsibility for change looks very different. Expectations and treatment within society may be largely responsible for the mental health issues faced by this community. When I teach my Psychology of Culture course—a class related to diversity, equity, and inclusion—I strive to bridge the experiences of the individual with the greater societal context. Early in the semester, active listening is one technique that I believe sets the table for the balance between one's individual needs and those of the whole. In this chapter, I'll try to walk you through a classroom experience that I later turned into an activity that I believe complements restorative practices.

I have a particular poem at hand that works well with students, "Refugees" by Brian Bilston.[1] The beginning of the active listening lesson starts something like this, "Okay, class, can someone read the poem aloud?" Nearly every time, there's a pause as the students try to wrap their mind around the task at hand as one brave person summons the courage to participate in a novel activity. I prompt them again, "Anyone? Come on, guys?" A male student begrudgingly responds, "I'll do it." With a smile I respond, "Thanks, Chris." (Chris is emblematic of any one of my community college students.)

After he reads the poem, I read it aloud from bottom to top. The majority of students straighten up in their seats as I jump down from my seated position on the desk. After reading the poem backward, I ask the class about the emotion evoked by the traditional top-to-bottom reading, then from the reversed bottom-to-top reading.

When read in the expected direction, the poem exudes emotions of anger, disgust, bigotry—and fear. In reverse, students shout out words like "hope," "disgust," "empathy," and "indignation." I have to poke and prod, but eventually the class recognizes that fear may also be at the root of their hope, disgust, empathy, and indignation. "They"—whatever group in society currently occupies this space—potentially fear that the refugees will be treated unjustly.

Bilston's poem turns on its side once again. At first, it was just a cool poem that could be read in both directions. Now the students are invited to consider that the person who believes the statement "cut-throats and thieves they are" is having the same emotional experience as the person stating "they are not cut-throats and thieves." It begs the question of

---

1 https://brianbilston.com/2016/03/23/refugees/

how political views and values can be so different yet fueled by similar emotions.

The attention-grabbing lesson hook has served its purpose. The students are intrigued, but they don't yet have a critical piece of information to connect the emphasis on emotion to active listening. This early in the course, emotions and cognition have mostly been described in biological terms that focus on the individual, but emotion can be the bridge between the needs of the individual and the needs of the collective.

As the lesson evolves, active listening will be proposed as the vehicle or tool required for constructive conversations related to issues of diversity. The next part of the lecture transitions into me revealing my reasoning for establishing a connection between emotion and active listening. The poem "Refugees" affords me the opportunity to explain a major tenet of my teaching philosophy early on in the semester. To establish this connection, I share with the class a memory about the way I felt in the wee hours of November 7, 2016—the morning Donald J. Trump won the election to be the forty-fifth president of the United States. Given the platform he ran on, I wondered what it would be like to be a diversity educator in this new America. When I arrived on campus the next day, my colleagues congregated outside my office door asking the same thing: How are you going to teach your culture class now? During the COVID-19 pandemic in 2020 and since the social shifts following a series of racial injustices sparked by the murder of George Floyd, I find myself asking a similar question: How will I now teach my culture classes when the world is focused, maybe even more polarized, on issues of police brutality within the African-American community? Back in 2016, my answer was active listening.

At heart, I am a psychologist: my training as a psychologist informs many of my actions as an educator. Therefore, the core conditions of counseling were at the top of my mind. Core conditions within counseling encompass the relationship that derives from person-centered therapy. They are described as both necessary and sufficient (Berven, Thomas, and Chan 2004, 3–16). "Sufficient" may seem less than satisfying, but the idea is that if a counselor practices the core aspects of counseling, the treatment will be curative with little additional intervention. Neither therapeutic orientation nor sophisticated intervention will ever take the place of the core conditions in counseling.

What I knew on November 7, 2016, was that the conversation and experience in my classroom was likely to shift in the coming semester. Throughout the presidential campaign, I had observed interactions on social media. People were not listening to one another. I was likely guilty of this when reading or hearing a viewpoint that failed to align with my sociopolitical stance. Although I abstained from the attacking behavior I observed so many engage in, I wondered how things might play out in a diversity-focused class. The bottom line was that communication seemed to consistently break down whether in print or in conversation. There was also a sense that individuals were avoiding sensitive conversations, fearing that an argument or name-calling would ensue. Some white folks feared being called racist; some people of color feared having to defend their traumatic existence. What was true in 2016 feels sadly similar in 2020.

As I considered the essential aspects that allow people to truly hear and listen to one another, I remembered one of the main tenets of Rogerian therapy—active listening. I thought about the poem "Refugees." The best way that I knew to be an effective diversity educator was to rely on my skills as a psychologist. I threw all my effort into the incorporation of active listening, hoping that if the top-to-bottom reader and the bottom-to-top reader of Bilston's poem could actually listen to one another's concerns and fears, then maybe, just maybe, our new America could make some progress.

What makes listening both active and reflective includes the "attempt to demonstrate unconditional acceptance and unbiased reflection" (Weger, Castle, and Emmett 2010). Within the fields of counseling and psychology, Carl Rogers is most closely associated with the concept of active or empathic listening (Corey 2015, 159). Active listening was developed by Gordon in 1975 but has roots in Rogers's 1951 conceptualization of empathic listening (Orlov 1992, 30, 36–41). Rogers is regarded as a major spokesperson and responsible for the creation of empathic listening as a psychotherapeutic technique (Corey 2015, 168). Active or empathic listening is based on unconditional acceptance and unbiased reflection of a client's experience (Weger, Castle, and Emmett 2010). "The goal in active listening is to develop a clear understanding of the speaker's concern and also to clearly communicate the listener's interest in the speaker's message" (McNaughton et al. 2008).

Active listening contains three essential elements: (1) the listener's nonverbal involvement, indicating full attention; (2) the listener's reflecting the message of the speaker back to him/her/them; and (3) the listener's questioning the speaker to encourage elaboration and further details (Weger, Castle, and Emmett 2010). Specific behavioral components of active listening include paraphrasing, focusing on both content and delivery, exerting significant effort as a participant in the conversation, communicating attentiveness through body language, and maintaining eye contact (Pearce, Johnson, and Barker 2003).

In my culture classes, I find it useful to break down the steps into five microskills that include paying attention, showing that you are listening, clarifying, deferring judgment, and responding appropriately. Levitt identifies active listening as a therapeutic microskill involving listening attentively and responding empathically so a client feels heard (Levitt 2002). Although microskills are important to learning any behavioral technique, they can feel awkward at first, even when, as here, they create the foundation for active listening.

Empathic listening is another way of referring to this invaluable technique. Empathic listening is frequently identified as a key communication skill for developing effective collaboration (O'Shea et al. 2000, 223). The goal is to communicate that the listener is doing their best to understand their partner's thoughts and feelings (empathy) and that the speaker's feelings are important to the listener (respect). Paying attention through eye contact is one of the first steps in connecting to another's emotion and demonstrating respect for what the individual is communicating. As simple as it seems to be present and put our phones down, many parents and educators experience daily struggles as they try to communicate with their kids. An additional challenge is that maintaining eye contact is based on one's culture and comfort.

Eye contact may foster intimacy for some. If two people are romantically interested in one another, flirtatious glances are a common way of communicating one's interest. To use a heteronormative example, women often find themselves engaged in either professional or everyday conversations with their male counterparts, and they may find themselves negotiating the length or intensity of their gaze for fear of unintentionally communicating romantic interest. Additionally, those from marginalized communities may have been instructed to look at someone in the eye when that person is speaking but to deflect their gaze when communicating. For example, at certain times in history, it was dangerous for African-Americans to make eye contact with white individuals. Direct eye contact could have been regarded as a challenge to the authority that supported racial supremacy. Although these dynamics have diminished and manifest differently today, implicit nonverbal communication is often passed down across generations. Therefore the instructions to listen and hold eye contact are complicated by one's identity and social status. In my active listening work with students, the discomfort or differences between eye contact are accepted.

Paying attention also requires that the listener mentally engage without preparing a rebuttal. Many feel that they need to have the next thought prepared and that a quick response is indicative of their intelligence. Others fear that if they don't keep their thought in mind, they will forget what to say when it is their chance to speak.

When we listen with our entire body, or listen fully, we have more of a tendency to remember what we have heard. When more senses are involved in learning, more potential exists to encode information. When we engage in the second step of empathic listening, responses are fuller and more authentic if we surrender to deeply hearing the other person. Deep listening includes gestures such as nodding, smiling, and using facial expressions to convey understanding, as well as sitting with an open posture and facing the speaker. When we practice this, students find these first two steps to be quite difficult because up to this point they are not allowed to verbally respond. At most, they may encourage the speaker to continue with small verbal comments such as "yes" or "uh-huh."

It takes time to get comfortable with holding back one's interjections and inflections. As one trains to become a psychologist, the revision of taped counseling sessions is essential to this process. When I was in my last year of residency, I learned to simply say "Mm" without offering more. The sound offered clients feedback. They knew that I was following their story without needing to verbally interrupt them. Admittedly, I don't speak this way when conversing with my family members. In our Cuban and Guatemalan family, we jump on top of one another's sentences and complete other people's phrases. But if the topic is serious, I use my active listening skills to ensure that my loved ones feel heard. It communicates the level of importance and respect for the shared content. Although my family is only one example, if I can learn to do this, my students can certainly endure a one-minute practice session where they attempt to listen without speaking.

After the first two steps are shared, students are asked to apply the learned skills with a prompt that has low stakes but is personal. For example, they may be asked to share where they came from. Students often share that listening only with the first two microskills feels artificial and forced because in a normal conversation they would provide a verbal response. I do my best to inform them that when the conversation is emotionally charged, both paying attention and listening with one's entire body are important steps that facilitate the listener's ability to truly hear; ideally, the listener will then connect with the passion beneath the speaker's argument. When the next prompt becomes more charged, they may have a deeper appreciation for these microskills.

Empathic listening allows you to prepare tailored responses. Paying attention to one's emotional or bodily reactions enables the listener to communicate genuine interest, understanding, and acceptance about the speaker's point of view. After the 2016 election, CNN correspondent Van Jones interviewed some of Trump's supporters. What Van Jones learned from his interviews was that Trump and Clinton supporters had the same fears and concerns as others. Some examples were a deep concern for ideas of liberty and justice. Additionally, feelings of fear over the loss of job opportunities and love and protection of family members were common concerns. His hypothesis was that those on the other side of the aisle needed to engage in deep listening and that the Democratic Party had ignored the concerns of white Americans of lower socioeconomic status. One of the goals of empathic listening is not to agree or disagree but simply to better understand the speaker's perspective (Turnbull and Turnbull 1990).

A teacher cannot really provide assistance to a student until they fully understand the problem (Covey 1989, 237). Whether counselors or educators are involved, many wish to effect a change in their students. Learning involves changing or adding to one's existing body of knowledge. Humanistic principles such as active listening create conditions for positive change. Active listening is identified as a core condition for change to occur. Although the field of psychology identifies active listening as a core condition for therapists, Rogers adopted the belief that the individual was the primary agent for constructive self-change (Bohart and Tallman 1999; Bozarth, Zimring, and Tausch 2002). Additionally, Rogers claimed that individuals were capable of learning these basic skills. He claimed that if people could learn these skills, practitioners would be able to focus on more severe mental health challenges. In essence, if folks listen to one another, their needs will be met, thus decreasing the need for professional help.

Let's get back to the steps of active listening and the students. Up to this point, they have learned essential microskills, but they feel bridled by their inability to verbally interact. The humanistic philosophy on which the person-centered approach rests is expressed in attitudes and behaviors that create a growth-producing climate. The third step offers the verbal skills that students crave. When they are allowed to clarify and check for understanding, the skill of active listening becomes more natural. This step includes reflecting back the speaker's words by paraphrasing what is shared.

Clarifying questions like "What do you mean when you describe your town as a hodgepodge of cultures?" allow the students to stay on topic and demonstrate to the speaker that the listener is engaged. Periodically summarizing comments affords the listener the ability to hear their own words. As simple as this sounds, it is one of the most effective facets of active listening. Saying something like "So, to make sure I got the main points, you said . . ." or "Did I miss anything?" provides an opportunity to correct one's own words or, better yet, to analyze the cause of one's feelings.

From the perspective of the listener, paying attention, listening with one's entire body, and posing clarifying questions enables them to become more in tune with their own emotional reactions. At this stage in the lesson on active listening, students are getting along and the conversations are benign enough for most people to feel comfortable with the discussion. Self-awareness of one's baseline of relaxed emotions is paramount to bridging the link between active listening and emotional awareness. Within this context, students are then instructed to practice with a prompt—though not one on the most controversial of current event topics—that may elicit a response.

For example, they may discuss the legalization of marijuana or a proposal to change the voting age. If they find themselves reacting emotionally, they are instructed to stop there and notice the emotion. If an individual is following the steps, the departure from their baseline emotion is often quite apparent. A sample verbal response may include "I may not be understanding you correctly, and I find myself taking what you said personally. What I thought you just said is . . . Is that what you meant?" This step results in the listener taking responsibility for their own emotional reaction instead of blaming their reaction on the speaker. Ideally, the listener will merely describe what they heard and abstain from offering interpretations. Interpretations are the analysis of what the speaker is or might be communicating.

According to Rogers (1951), this helps people develop their capacities and stimulates constructive change in others. Individuals are empowered, and they are able to use this power for personal and social transformations (Corey 2015, 164). Additionally, active listening fosters genuineness and acceptance. The more real, genuine, and authentic we are as educators, the more our students can model this behavior (Corey 2015, 169). By fully listening to others, one demonstrates a deep and genuine caring, creating an unconditional, positive regard for those that we communicate with.

The last two steps of active listening, deferring judgment and responding appropriately, prepare students for their toughest practice round as they attempt to apply the skills. One of the most powerful exchanges I ever observed occurred between two female students. One was a young woman from Mexico who was a DACA recipient. The other student was a white female whose grandfather had been killed by a drunk driver who was undocumented. These two women truly heard one another. As difficult as it was, they allowed one another to finish their points before asking questions. Although one student literally had to sit on her hands, she was able to curb her desire to interrupt with a counterargument. Both women were able to respond openly, honestly, and respectfully.

Similar to Van Jones's conclusions about the interviews of Trump voters, these two young women were able to discuss the motivations and reasons for their beliefs instead of attacking one another for their point of view. When asked to provide feedback to their peers, they were able to agree to disagree on their political conclusions, but they were also able to connect over their love for their individual family members. The two students embodied the "Refugees" poem. One was looking at the situation from the top down, the other from the bottom up. Fear and pain over their lived experiences could have skewed their exchange, but the ability to express and harness their emotions through the skills of active listening proved to be a restorative practice.

PAY ATTENTION.

- Hold eye contact, if it's appropriate with everyone's culture and comfort.
- Be present and avoid distractions.
- Just listen, without preparing a rebuttal so that you can retain better memories of what you've heard and be able to give a tailored response.

LISTEN WITH YOUR BODY.

- Maintain an open and inviting posture by
  ◦ facing the speaker,
  ◦ nodding,
  ◦ smiling,
  ◦ and using other facial expressions.
- Encourage the speaker to continue with small verbal cues such as
  ◦ "yes"
  ◦ and "uh-huh."
- Pay attention to your physical or emotional reactions.

CLARIFY AND CHECK FOR UNDERSTANDING.

- Reflect back by paraphrasing with phrases like
  ◦ "What I'm hearing is . . .";
  ◦ "Did I miss anything?";
  ◦ "It sounds like you are saying . . .";
  ◦ and "Am I understanding you correctly?"
- Use questions to clarify, asking things like "What do you mean when you say . . .?"
- Periodically summarize comments.
- If you find yourself reacting emotionally to own your reaction, stop and say, "I may not be understanding you

correctly, and I find myself taking what you said personally. What I thought you just said is . . . Is that what you meant?"

DEFER JUDGMENT.

- Allow the speaker to finish each point before asking questions.
- Don't offer interpretations, because your analysis of what the speaker is saying or why they might be saying it is not part of listening to them.

RESPOND APPROPRIATELY.

- Be open and honest in your response, and respectfully assert opinions by talking about yourself and your motivations.
- Avoid interrupting with counterarguments or attacking, which can feel disrespectful and result in frustration, defeating the goal of understanding.

GIVE FEEDBACK.

- Discuss how what you've heard has helped you with phrases like
  - "The most helpful part of your reflecting/paraphrasing was . . ."
  - or "The most helpful parts of your clarifying questions were . . . They made me feel . . ."
- Offer constructive thoughts from your own perspective with phrases like "It would help me open up or feel listened to more if . . ."

A NOTE ON OBSERVATION
FROM MARISOL

The concept of active observation is pretty simple. It's been referred to as educators having "with-it-ness," being aware of what's going on with students. This is simply taking note of verbal cues and non-verbal actions and responding to them. You need to be aware of what is being communicated to you through behavior. With time, you get a general sense of people's natural dispositions. By observing, you can tune into changes. Does the person you're listening to look tired? More excited than usual? Quieter than normal? By noticing changes, you can check in with your community members.

As a teacher, I would stand by the door to welcome students. That was the perfect moment to greet them, welcome them to our time together, and do an observational check. The same was true when I was a school principal. Walking the halls and stepping into classrooms allowed me to greet, connect, and check in with staff. Actively observing allows you to be cued in to the social and emotional wellness of others.

Recently the power of observation became very clear to me during extended time at home with my family. One morning, Daniel told me that he was temporarily assigned a new supervisor. When he shared this with me, I was in the middle of something and pushed it out of my mind. To me this was no big deal; he is an amazing social worker who is constantly being recognized for his work, attention to detail, and care of clients.

His desk is in the living room, and as I moved about my day, I began to notice his leg shaking. A lot. I stopped and asked if he was stressed. He responded with, "Of course I'm stressed. I have a new supervisor." So we talked and kept talking. This incident taught me to pay attention to more than just what I hear but to observe and provide space for my loved ones to process, if that is what is needed.

Both active listening and observing are skills that need to be practiced in a restorative culture. During circles/círculos and check-in/check-out, it's important to remember to pay attention to all that is being communicated both verbally and nonverbally. The framework provided by Dr. Lafaurie is critical to practice and master.

— CHAPTER SEVEN —

Trauma and Resilience

BY

Dr. Carolyn Gery

AWARENESS REQUIRES SELF-UNDERSTANDING AND ACCEPTANCE. IT REQUIRES WORK.

—Donna Hicks, PhD

When I started to write this chapter, I was sitting in a coffee shop, hands wrapped around a hot cup of coffee, admiring a bright-blue sky on a cold winter morning. My office at home sat empty, quiet, and abandoned. I chose the noise of others, strangers whose voices provided a soft background to my thinking. We are, at our core, herd animals.

The first word I wrote, "trauma," seemed out of place when I typed it; the word did not fit the warmth and comfort of the café. Yet I knew, through my research and experience, that my fellow coffee sippers had most likely experienced some level of trauma at one point or at multiple points in their lives. Looking at each face, I realized I did not know the stories behind the expressions, but I did know trauma is our invisible shadow, integrated into our being, sometimes on glorious display but most often lurking in the nuances of our lives, a soft gray that shades our interactions and reactions.

Now, working on the last few sentences of the chapter, it is May 2020, and I reflect how in a few short months, the world has changed dramatically. In the midst of a pandemic, there is no choice but to work from home; the option of a café filled with the buzz of its patrons seems so far away. I am writing with my close friend, the primary author of this book. We meet almost daily—virtually—and share the ins and outs of our lives, then "together" we write, her music providing the soundtrack for our new normal. Although it is not the same as being physically present, I am still drawn to the company of others.

The collective experience of the pandemic makes me realize the universal impact of trauma on a global community. I am cognizant of the disparate ways the experience makes its mark on each person, dependent upon the factors present or not present in their lives to mitigate the harmful effects of the crisis. The emergent reality is a person, already traumatized, who enters into a traumatic situation, making that person much more vulnerable. Yet, even now, hope can be found in the acts of kindness and selflessness many are showing others. In the midst of a global crisis, people are reaching out to connect, support, and offer solace. The power of the human spirit is indeed mighty, and in its purest form, a relationship with another has the capacity to buffer many of the harmful, debilitating effects of trauma.

How do we leverage the power of the human spirit to support each other during a crisis, both at a personal and community level? And when a traumatic event passes, how do we continue to support, nurture, and protect each other so that we are able to heal ourselves and our communities? We start by acknowledging how we are all interconnected and tied to each other through relationships. The path forward is an integrated, comprehensive approach honoring the delicate bond between one and another, between one person and a community, and this approach strengthens this bond with an intent to create resilience.

A resilient culture is able to create the requisite support systems to house restorative practices. Resilience is the capacity to bounce back after adversity; it is the rubber-band effect, and the elasticity inherent in this effect is the flexibility of the culture to adapt, to flex with a situation, and to respond in ways that make the culture stronger. Defined more fully, resiliency is the "ability to identify and use individual and collective strengths to live fully in the present moment and to thrive while managing the tasks of daily living" (Miller-Karas 2015, 6). Resiliency provides safety and the space for members to make themselves vulnerable as healing conversations take place.

Healing is an integral part of this process; it is what provides the space for resilience to thrive. Restorative healing operates with the intention of having a culture able to acknowledge and make reparations when harm has been done, either to an individual or to the whole community. To understand hurt and harm, to dig below the surface of conflict with the purpose of understanding the root cause of pain, requires a trauma-informed lens at the individual and community levels. This perspective acknowledges the relationship between conflict and unaddressed behavior. "Trauma shapes overall behavior including patterns of wrongdoing and conflict as well as processes of recovery, resolution, or transformation. The social as well as the individual dimensions of trauma must be addressed as part of peacebuilding and restorative justice processes" (Zehr 2008, 10).

A cycle exists where unhealed and unaddressed trauma, at both the individual and collective levels, becomes the catalyst of behaviors that are often seen as disruptive, damaging, and hurtful. The behavior is what is seen and felt by a community, but what is not immediately apparent is the root cause of the action or reaction. It is not knowing, not understanding the root cause of behavior, that can cause hurt within a community. This can form the basis of miscommunication and misunderstanding, resulting in a divide between members and causing damage to another or the community as a whole. To only address the visible mark, the action, and ignore the root cause is to dress a wound without first cleaning the surface; repairing the emotional fear underlying the physical pain must come first. The harm is at the relational level, where the power generated by the belief we have in each other is diminished by hurt, miscommunication, and anger.

Creating a space for healing to occur requires you, the individual, to openly understand your personal relationship with unresolved hurt, pain, and conflict. We all hurt, and this unifying experience creates an empathetic bridge between you and others. To heal is to be vulnerable; to commit to healing as a community is to engage with restorative practices, which are built for the sole purpose of creating peace—for each other, for our relationships, and for our world.

UNDERSTANDING HOW TRAUMA IMPACTS RELATIONSHIPS

There are many elements in play within this dynamic. The foundation is built upon a culture of respect and knowledge gained through a deep social-emotional awareness. The capacity to look honestly at oneself and the impact of self upon and within the community provides the lens to discern when individual action has community impact, either positively or negatively. This foundation is the hardest to measure. There is the individual's social-emotional awareness and also the collective understanding of the culture as a whole. This awareness is able to forge solid values that have the power to guide the culture and act as a North Star to gauge disruption and mediate arising conflict.

You can't build a positive culture, a safe, nurturing community where all thrive, without constructing ways to exist as a member of that collective of identities gathering in your space every day. Your job as a member of the community is structured and defined by rules, accepted norms, and metrics to determine success. Yet what is not always measured is the relational strength of a community providing the capacity to grow, to become more resilient, and in the process, to be more flexible in handling the inevitabilities of life. The power of a collective, the potential to learn not just from you but from others grappling with hard work, real problems, is a wieldy tool. It is belonging, the "I get you" and "you get me." Unspoken but understood.

Can you have learning, deep learning that translates into the actualization of every mission statement, if you do not know each other? Are you able to knit together the strengths, insights, and powers of being actors in the system, if you do not trust each other? It is the relational capacity of the community member that provides the connection: the connection between the teacher and the student, between colleagues, and the community to the leader. The common variable is you. So let's start there. And let's talk about the hard stuff. We all hurt, process pain, and experience levels of discomfort. This is our common link, that which makes us human and connects us to each other.

Although invisible, trauma is prevalent among us. According to a landmark study from the Centers of Disease Control and Prevention, a large segment of our population has experienced what is referred to as an adverse childhood experience, or ACE. The findings analyzed data from 9,508 participants and found that "more than half of respondents reported at least one, and one-fourth reported (greater than) 2 categories of exposure" (Felitti et al. 1998, 245).

Trauma is personal and directly linked to how one's emotional and physical state is compromised by an experience. In Elaine Miller-Karas's book, *Building Resilience to Trauma*, trauma is defined as a reaction unique to the individual:

> Trauma can be defined in many ways, but, most importantly, it is *an individual's perception of an event as threatening to oneself or others*. An event that results in trauma for one person may not be experienced by another individual as traumatic. Even if every member of a family experiences the same event, each may have a different perspective regarding the event.

The experience of trauma impacts our psychological and physical well-being long after a specific event or well into adulthood, if the event was recurrent in one's childhood. This imprint can resurface in many ways, for instance, as threats, causing the brain and physiological system to respond, and it actually impacts the "feeling of being alive" (Van der Kolk 2014).

Trauma, in this context, is our emotional and physical response to an experience that overwhelmed us. This could be one event, or an ongoing experience that caused our system to go into a fight, flight, or freeze reaction. The sense of being overwhelmed has biological, emotional, behavioral, spiritual, and even societal consequences that can persist if not healed. The original sensation resurfaces when we are triggered, something not always understood by the person who causes the uncomfortable connection. At this point, there is a disconnection that leads to a reaction seen as transgression and unwarranted behavior. Understanding the role of trauma as an integral part of conflict is important, especially as you come to a common agreement about the conflict. It is still a personal translation of the harm, housed within your own operating definition of what defines conflict, justice, and, essentially, right and wrong.

When we think of ourselves as part of a larger whole—a school, community, or other organization—it is important to recognize that trauma operates at the individual and collective levels *at the same time*. We are individuals who make sense of our worlds through our own histories and experiences. This lens influences how we relate to others, it impacts the relationships we form with other individuals as colleagues and friends, and it affects how we mediate our relationships with groups of people in the social networks we inhabit. Understanding the potential influence trauma has in impacting our relational capacity to develop and nurture healthy relationships will provide us with an informed awareness of the mindset we bring to difficult community discussions.

HEALING TRAUMA:
THE CORE INGREDIENTS

A community capable of leveraging restorative practices to build, strengthen, and support a more resilient culture through a trauma-informed lens requires three attributes: a commitment to be a learning community, a high level of trust, and collective efficacy. These are the mighty superpowers, the equivalent of seeing the invisible while leaping over any obstacle.

A community that learns together, grows together. A community has a common identity and exists due to the ability of group members to mutually create a shared practice and collectively engage in learning (Wenger 1998). The use of the word "community" to define a group of practitioners working as a cohesive unit denotes the existence of shared identity as well as a nonstatic state-of-being. There is life and growth within the group that permeates the relationships and structures of learning. Understanding a new approach and working with new practices involves trying, failing, succeeding, and—always—reflecting.

Learning does not happen in silos. Organizations are stronger when all are included in processes, regardless of individuals' roles or experiences. Members belonging to a learning community are unified by a common set of practices, a shared way of knowing, and the inclusion of both experts and novices engaged in accomplishing similar goals (Riel and Fulton 2001). Community members are recognized for what they know as well as what they need to learn. Vander Ark (2004) further delineates the characteristics of a professional learning community as one that "shares and exhibits a set of commitments, beliefs, and practices, which result in candor, collaboration, and coherence toward adult and student learning" (6). It is this capacity to be vulnerable, to not have the answers, to be open to learning and exploring a practice that will provide the power to apply restorative practices authentically.

Learning happens best if there is a way to fail safely; this is how resilience is built. When working with new practices at a community level, trust in each other provides the space to be your most vulnerable, to reflect on how to improve, and to know when to ask for help. In the context of a teacher community, trust is defined as the collective belief that teachers can rely on the integrity of their colleagues; it can be measured by the extent the group is willing to risk vulnerability (Tschannen-Moran and Hoy 1997, 334–352). Trust is not something that is easy to create, maintain, or sustain. Yet it is trust that opens the door for the most difficult conversations to take place. When trust permeates every facet of a community, it becomes a safety net.

The third critical ingredient is the overriding belief in the power of the group to learn, to trust, and to meet the challenge of creating a more peaceful community. "Collective" refers to the degree that group members have a consensus regarding their capacity to achieve change; it is influenced by the existence of relational trust. The belief in the capacity of the group as a whole feeds the hope needed to create resiliency in a culture. Efficacy is a solid force within a culture when the pervasive feeling is "together, we can do this!" Collective efficacy promotes resiliency and works to disarm the effect of trauma. It is essentially a protective factor.

UNDERSTANDING OUR NARRATIVE HELPS US BUILD TRUST

We tell stories for making sense, to convey ourselves to others, and to connect. Communities have their own stories that connect all in a shared reality. It's a way to express what you need and to invite those around you to share in your experience. Howard Zehr (2008) states, "Personal and communal narratives—story and 're-storying'—play critical roles in conflict resolution, trauma recovery, and restorative justice, and opportunities for storytelling must be incorporated into our processes" (5). Stories define an individual, create links to others, and also add to the overall tapestry of a culture. As we listen to each other, authentically and without judgment, we operate with an empathetic mindset. With empathy, you can create the interconnected responsibility to do the hard work of restorative practice. The demonstration of empathy and the acceptance of its product also builds trust. Through a personal narrative, one finds a tool to explore traumatic events and to work through the actions resulting in harm to a community.

To frame it, I'm going to share a story with you. We will examine an experience, explore the role of trauma, and look at how a community open to learning and willing to trust, with collective belief in each member, can become stronger.

DR. GERY, YOUR AURA FOLLOWED YOU INTO THE GYM

It was a burnt-toast morning. Me against the universe, and I was several points behind. Waking up tired, no cream for my coffee, could not find clothes to fit my uncomfortable mood, and every stoplight heightened my theory that I had stepped into some really bad karma that was definitely not of my own making. My mind was fuzzy, and the caffeinated edge was not softening the memory of a restless night, awake at every hour, unsettled.

As the principal of a small K–8 school, I would start each day with a whole-school morning meeting. It was a way to begin the school day together, a time to shout out celebrations and discuss our work and ways of being, and a chance for me to gauge the temperature of the day. Surveying the room, I would take note of tired, blank stares from staff, students who were jumpy and disheveled, and the figurative and literal collective sound our culture was emitting. This is how I would set up my schedule for the morning: have tea with students, check in on staff, find resources for families, and connect staff to other staff for extra support. This was also a time for staff to see me, to have a routine, show off their news from their classes, and for our whole community to come together, celebrate, tell stories, inform, and start our day.

That day, I was rushed. I wasn't able to get myself settled into the morning, and I felt I was already running behind. Looking at the clock, I was irritated. Why do I never seem to have enough time? How was I going to get through the morning? I had a list larger than the hours in the day and no sense of how I was going to break it apart. Go, I told myself, now—you are running late.

The school gymnasium was much louder than usual, and I noted it was that time of year, right before winter break, when the school felt like an airplane before takeoff, engines revving and not enough tarmac for full lift-off. But I made it work, I kept us going, and twenty minutes later I was back in my office—staring at my unanswered emails. Phew! I made it! Or so I thought.

Dominic, our art teacher, came in and sat down. He looked at me and asked how I was doing. "Fine," I said. There was a pause. "Okay—it's been a rough morning." He said, "Your aura followed you into the gym today and I wanted to check in on you and see if there is anything I can do to help."

I literally shrank into my chair.

"I thought I had it handled," I said. Inside, my heart choked. I am the leader, I chided myself, everyone looks to me for guidance. How could I have been the one to shade our morning in a darker color?

This is why: I had had a sleepless night—one added to many sleepless nights over the last few months. I was struggling with our school budget; our revenue from the state kept dropping, and I would look at every line item to see if there was some way to find some breathing space. I had to keep it together, and I shared my worry with no one. This was what was instilled in me from an early age when, at almost three, I lost my father, who died of an unexpected and undetected brain aneurysm. In my three-year-old world, he did not come home one day, and I did not know why.

My mother, my sister, and I moved across the country, urn in tow, and settled into a house next to a freeway. My older sister, who had Down syndrome, would run repeatedly into the street. My mom would frantically trail after her while my sister laughed joyfully, a big grin on her face. Soon, she was placed in a home, and it was determined it would be best if I had no contact with her as she transitioned to her new situation. Another loss.

I grew into the responsible one. My mom leaned on me when she was anxious, fearful, or when money was tight, and she looked to me to be calm when she was unable to hold it together. At my core, I believed if I just worked harder, worked smarter, I could figure out a way to fix things. This was how I confronted past challenges and struggles, but I realized, in my role as principal, this no longer worked for me. I was completely overwhelmed and felt like a failure, and I felt I was fail-ing the school—during a recession when the end was not in sight and grants were even more difficult to find, my hard work was not translat-ing into relief.

The impact of loss, fiscal insecurity, constant mobility, and absorb-ing the stress of an anxious parent played out in my life in the following ways: unrelenting insomnia, anxiety, and placing work above personal health. There is a tendency for many who have experienced traumatic events to have a higher degree of addictive behaviors, health issues, and trouble with establishing relationships (Felitti et al. 1998, 246). Trauma showed up in me as the tendency to be a workaholic and to sleep poorly.

While I was struggling to make sure the school survived, I was con-sumed with finding a way to find additional financial resources. I was awake many evenings, poring over the budget, examining and reexam-ining each line item to see how I could minimize impact on the staff and students. I was also constantly researching grant resources, applying for funding, and working to connect with potential donors. To me, it felt like I had some level of control. What I didn't realize was that it was slowly taking a toll on my health and emotional resilience.

Dominic was able to see a change in my demeanor when I was unable to acknowledge the effect stress was having on me. It was hard to have this pointed out to me, yet it was important that someone addressed the issue. I realized in that moment I was not creating a cul-ture of safety and respect if I was unable to model how to reach out for support when I was struggling. I took the moment to open up and share my concern, my worry about the budget, and why this challenge shook me to my core. He sat there, still, quiet, and listening.

When I stopped speaking, he responded, "Okay—don't you think together we can shoulder this?"

"Yes," I agreed. "I do."

We, as a whole school, navigated those waters together. We did it without layoffs and got creative with grants, with networking, and through a true collaboration with our parent community. A new struc-ture reorganized our week to have time together each Friday to analyze our data, brainstorm, share celebrations, and plan our next week. This time was held as sacred and it started in a circle. Each member of our school had a chance to discuss a challenge, including myself. We learned to listen, to not solve in the moment, and to provide support for each other. Trust was how we worked through interpersonal conflicts with each other: directly and with kindness. Trust showed up when we honored what was shared, clarified when we did not understand, and talked about hurt and fear when these feelings emerged.

Recognizing the impact of a traumatic experience on your being is a monumental act requiring a deep awareness of your social and emotional well-being. Locating this in the context of a public space where you operate in a specific role places you in a vulnerable position. This is especially apparent when you acknowledge, verbally, your emotions and specifically how you are feeling. Trust has to be present to ensure one is not sacrificing your own healing for the good of the community. Trust in the culture and in the commitment to be an organization.

It was not perfect. Yet we were committed to our students, our families, and one another. We believed in the power of our culture, and we were determined to do the hard work of facing our failures openly—this was the only way we could learn. Through this process, I learned to be a better communicator. Open, honest, without bravado and drama. This is how we built trust during a time of struggle, when the future of our school appeared very fragile. By creating a space to be vulnerable, we became stronger.

Analyzing your own experiences and the experiences of the community as a whole creates a collective understanding of the impact these experiences have on developing a culture open and supportive of healing. The process provides members within the community the opportunity to understand the connection between trauma and one's ability to build resilience. In the article "Strategies for Trauma Awareness and Resilience Programme: experiential education towards resilience and trauma informed people and practice," Kathryn Mansfield states, "While deep technical expertise is helpful for understanding and responding to trauma and (re)building resilience, basic knowledge and awareness can provide a substantial foundation for communities and individuals, whether or not they hold such technical expertise" (Mansfield 2017, 264). When trust is in the room, stories flow and connections flourish. Belonging is created where there is security, dignity, and the capacity to build a working, shared definition of justice. It is all about relationships.

— CHAPTER EIGHT —

Responding To Challenges

A ll new practices, initiatives, and movements bring excitement and challenges. The latter can show up in the form of barriers and resistance. It's important to honor that this is a natural reaction to change. It can be hard to understand why everyone is not as excited and energized as you are about deepening the connection with students and colleagues. When you accept this as part of the process, you can prepare to deal with the barriers, roadblocks, and challenges that will come. We believe that part of this preparation includes foreseeing barriers and understanding their origins. This section will provide insight into common struggles that educators face when introducing restorative practices.

The challenging behaviors addressed in this chapter are not all inclusive and are not limited to schools. By addressing these behaviors, we are not calling out or placing blame on educators. These behaviors exist wherever human beings exist. Please read through the descriptions and recommendations with an open heart, and know that they are intended to support all sides of the challenge. If you see yourself, or a beloved team or family member, in these descriptors, this is a gift. Reflection and acceptance are steps into the process of growth and healing.

REFUSAL TO ENGAGE IN CIRCLES/ CÍRCULOS AND COMMUNITY BUILDING

At its core, restorative practices are the way in which we connect and build community. This way of discussing and sharing can be difficult. So difficult, in fact, that some students or adults don't fully engage or participate. In the circle, there is space and room to meet everyone exactly where they are. When introducing restorative practices, it's important to reinforce that this way of being is centuries old and helps build community and connection. This is not about forcing relationships, but it is an opportunity to relate to one another in a deeper way. If you have a participant that flat- out refuses to participate, proceed with love and clarity about the purpose for this way of being. Establishing trust is essential, especially with those who are hesitant.

SUGGESTIONS FOR RESPONDING

If you notice that someone is not engaging or self-identifies as not wanting to participate in sharing, you have options for including them as part of the process.

Acknowledge their honesty and ability to identify their needs. This shows reflection and ownership of emotions and readiness. These qualities are exactly what we hope for in ourselves and community members. Let them know that participation as a community member during the circle/círculo is required, as they are important members, but each member's participation can look different depending on their needs.

All participants have the option of passing when it comes their turn to share. But they must remain in the circle/círculo and commit to listening with their hearts to all others. If someone is not able to sit in the circle, they can participate as an active observer responsible for listening and then provide a short summary to the group before the circle/ círculo closes. Set up a seat outside of the circle, let participants know of this process, and provide the observer with a prompt that is linked to the purpose of the circle/círculo.

SEE THE RESOURCES CHAPTER FOR SAMPLE
PROMPTS FOR ACTIVE OBSERVERS.

Be gentle with those who need more time to trust the work that happens in circles/círculos while remaining firm in your organization's commitment to this way of being.

DISCOMFORT WITH SHARING PERSONAL HISTORY OR EXPERIENCES

In Greek mythology, when the demigod Achilles was a baby, his mother Thetis tried to make him immortal by dipping him in the magical River Styx. The river provided the power of invulnerability to those who bathed in its waters. Thetis held on to Achilles's heel as she dipped him into the powerful waters. Every part of his body was protected except for the space where his mother held his heel with her thumb and finger. Achilles became a great warrior and appeared immortal. The story tells us that while at war with the Trojans, the god Apollo guided an arrow to the spot on Achilles's heel where his mother held him, causing his death.

This story teaches us that no matter how strong anyone appears, we can be hurt or harmed. You may be faced with a community member who openly states that they are uncomfortable sharing their personal stories. Sharing takes courage in the form of vulnerability. Some people are also very private and may sound like my daughter who says that she "hates people knowing my business." Modeling vulnerability and authenticity can help others who are hesitant be willing to try. Establishing trust will open the door for more people to share their stories. At the root of the reluctance to share is the belief that vulnerability is a weakness.

Sharing in circles/círculos can lead to revealing joyful, painful, loving, tender, sad, disheartening, and hopeful experiences. These experiences expose so much about us—what motivates us, what's important to us, what can harm us, what we love, and what we fear. Talking about our intimate experiences can lead to anxiety and tears. Some of us are taught that revealing these things is akin to revealing our most vulnerable weaknesses or Achilles' heels. Some may not want to be perceived as weak by their students, colleagues, parents, and supervisors. When we make the choice to be vulnerable in this way, we open ourselves up to the possibility of someone using sensitive information against us.

SUGGESTIONS FOR RESPONDING

Being vulnerable takes courage and strength. By being vulnerable, we allow for our true emotions and experiences to be processed and honored. Our most authentic selves live in the brave space of vulnerability. By sharing in this way, we open the possibility for true human connection. This connection is where the magic of community is conceived.

When you commit to restorative practices, you walk in this life with an authentic heartset and mindset. This means that you create trusting relationships with people and are able to discern between those who value this way of being and those who don't. The way forward in this work is to be vulnerable and share your experiences, thoughts, and emotions. Every time I've shared deep, dark pain and shame—the emotions I struggle with the most, especially as connected to parenting—I've had multiple members of my community reach out and thank me for opening the door for them to share their own pain, fear, and shame.

It's important to acknowledge and show gratitude for a person's ability to reflect and accept that it is hard for them to share stories and emotions. When giving a prompt that could provoke emotion, volunteer to be the first to share. This communicates trust to your community. It always helps others give themselves permission to brave discomfort. You can ask participants to first respond to prompts about vulnerability in a journal then move into a circle, where participants share their responses.

> SEE THE RESOURCES CHAPTER FOR SAMPLE
> PROMPTS ABOUT VULNERABILITY.

STUDENTS AND STAFF WHO MAY BE NEEDIER, MORE SELF-ABSORBED, OR MORE NEGATIVE

There are personalities that can be challenging. The most difficult ones are those who may be negative, extremely needy, or self-absorbed. They are challenging because they require a lot of attention, and others around them may feel provoked and then react. These reactions may range from becoming negative themselves to dismissing the person, allowing the person to absorb a lot of time and energy, or ignoring or ostracizing the person. All of these reactions disrupt the flow of the work.

WHAT TO LOOK FOR

A negative personality may say things like:

- "Restorative practices will never work. This was tried at the school where my husband teaches, and students just learned to manipulate admin and got away with everything."
- "I'm here to teach, not to share personal things about my life with students."
- "We already do so much; now we're expected to take time out of our learning time to facilitate circles/círculos? I just won't do it."

Look for people who aren't engaging in the practices. The extremely needy person may be overly emotional; take up a lot of talking time; constantly seek validation; or run to someone who is upset to comfort them and start talking over them, instead of allowing the speaker their time to share and process. The self-absorbed person may act very much like the needy person but will also try to redirect all conversations back to themselves, their students, their classroom; not be listening when others are sharing; or try to respond directly to others who are sharing with an experience of their own.

SUGGESTIONS FOR RESPONDING

View these personalities as the gift that they are to you and to the school community. I love when these difficult personalities show up because then I know what I'm working with, and I can make efforts to connect with them.

Remember that every person deserves to be heard. Honor the dignity of each person and provide them space to share. Everyone's experience deserves validation.

Reinforce agreements regarding "I statements," listening, and not responding to others' comments. You can change or add agreements as needed.

Discuss participation from an objective perspective. You can share observations about who you see speaking first or last. Discuss what it means to speak up and then step down, allowing others the opportunity to share. Practice active empathetic listening and discuss what it feels like to listen and what it feels like to be listened to.

If you have a staff member refusing to guide circles/círculos, set a minimum expectation of practices and check-ins. Then cofacilitate with the staff member. Debrief and provide feedback.

Remember that the key to all success is relationships.

PERCEPTION THAT STUDENTS AND STAFF ARE NOT HELD ACCOUNTABLE FOR THEIR BEHAVIOR

Restorative practices are a way for harm to be repaired. This is done through dialogue in the form of circles and mediation. Engaging in this eliminates the traditional disciplinary system where perpetrators of harmful acts are given a punishment by an authority figure. Most educators were raised and started their careers in educational systems that, for the most part, approached behavior with a deficit response. This response includes harsh and even extreme consequences that are related to the offense or series of offenses committed by the perpetrator.

Moving away from a punitive hierarchical system of discipline can be a hard change for members of the school community.

Restorative practices work because they provide a way for each member of the school community to truly connect with themselves and each other through listening and sharing of the individual and collective human experience. By taking responsibility for harm that has occurred and by expressing the impact of that harm, individuals and communities break down the walls of judgment and the othering that occurs.

I've heard and witnessed incidents that legitimize complaints about the implementation of restorative practices. When not implemented as a way of being, this work can be perceived as a way for manipulative adults and students to get away with horrifying and/or violent behavior. It can seem that all they have to do is talk in a circle with the appearance of sincerity and apologize before they can return to school the next day with no repercussions. A good friend of mine worked in a school system where this was the case. At his school site, a series of violent fights between students resulted in physical injuries to them and the staff. He reported to me that the principal, who claimed to be a restorative practitioner, held a meeting with the individual students and their parents/guardians. Each student returned to the school. There was no mediation between the parties that caused harm to each other nor was there any mediation with the students and staff who were injured. No one at the school site received any information about the incident or how the harm caused would be repaired. While this administrator gathered staff for a morning circle/círculo every morning that sometimes included students, they were not enacting truly restorative practices, and they were not using all the ways of the practice that could have transformed their school system. If the school was truly restorative, then all impacted parties would have the opportunity to dialogue about the event and have a say in how trust was damaged by harm, which could then be repaired.

Whenever I hear the concern that it seems that restorative practices equal no accountability for behavior, I investigate and discover that the issue has to do with implementation and not the practice itself. This is not something that you simply do from time to time; it is a way of being and connecting.

SUGGESTIONS FOR RESPONDING

This is a very difficult challenge to respond to because the people in the system may believe that they are truly employing restorative practices. An audit of practices or connecting and consulting with a restorative practices expert may be needed. While there is a cost associated with bringing in an outside expert, their work should result in a clear plan of action for full implementation that will ultimately transform the system for years to come, making this a wise investment. The expert should be able to establish a trusting and safe space for all members to bravely reengage with this work. The consultant should review data with system leaders and meet with members of the community to facilitate circles/círculos with the aim to identify both what is working and areas in need of growth. The expert should then be able to provide additional training; coach and provide feedback to all levels of staff; and guide all staff to commit to the practices. An outcome of this should be a process detailing how staff and parents will be informed of the agreements made during mediation. This information should include how and when actions will be taken to repair harm. By the end of the contract, the system should have what it needs to bring full and true implementation of restorative practices.

If there is no change, the system must acknowledge that there is no authentic commitment to restorative practices. Members of the system can then decide if they want to truly be restorative and go through the recommended process, or they can choose not to do this. If they choose not to do this, they should not claim to be a restorative system.

ADULT COMFORT WITH RUNNING CIRCLES/CÍRCULOS

Restorative practices require planning and awareness of issues impacting the community. This is a space where proficient facilitators can prevent issues and harm from occurring by addressing tension or topics that can cause disharmony and discord. It's also a space where others can be elevated and recognized. Participating in circles/círculos can be challenging, even for your most effective and seasoned teachers. This work is different because you're guiding and tending to people's experiences and emotions.

Some adults may struggle with the idea of guiding and facilitating circles/círculos or mediation. This turmoil can prevent circles/círculos from ever starting. A restorative community embeds a time for circles, check-in/check-out, and mediation every day and as needed. The more adults are engaged, the more comfortable they will be in leading this work with their students or staff.

SUGGESTIONS FOR RESPONDING

If you still have adults who are hesitant or nervous about starting this work with their staff or students, there are ways you can support their capacity in this work.

Cofacilitate circles/círculos. Meet with hesitant staff to plan for the circle/círculo and decide on roles. Provide feedback focusing on their strengths. Once they are facilitating on their own, sit in to provide feedback on growth and observations of effective practice.

Provide additional training to staff and build this training time into the school/organization budget. Training can include sitting in with other facilitators to observe. You can also provide resources in the form of prepared questions, practice, and feedback. If you have a number of staff who are hesitant, pair them up with a mentor teacher to work with them. Another approach is to engage in a circle/círculo focused on the facilitation of restorative practices.

SEE THE RESOURCES CHAPTER FOR FACILITATING
RESTORATIVE PRACTICES CIRCLES/CÍRCULOS.

INAPPROPRIATE BOUNDARIES

My children are the driving force for my life, in all ways. Because of them, I want to be the best woman possible. In my perspective, this means embracing growth, being financially independent, engaging in my spiritual practice, helping others, and only engaging in loving and respectful relationships that honor my dignity. Because I want to be the best person possible, I also want the same for them. This means doing the right thing. Sometimes the right thing means telling my daughters no, even when it breaks my heart to disappoint them. At some point, my heart accepted that my children weren't always going to like me, and that was okay, as long as I was acting from the best place of love possible.

This way of being with my girls transferred to the classroom. When I entered teaching, at twenty-five, my daughters were five and four years old. I entered the classroom understanding that while I wanted to be liked by my students, it was more important for me to do right by them, and doing the right thing can make an adolescent not like you very much.

I was blessed with beautiful friendships. The friendship that I've shared with Atiya since we were kids has been key to the development of my self-esteem and sense of value. We are all human beings who at our core want to be seen, heard, liked, and loved. And when that happens, it makes us feel good. In almost every school system in which I've worked, I've found adults who maintained inappropriate boundaries with students. These staff did things so that students would like them. Most of these adults are really caring people who just could not tell students no. Some of them suffered from low self-esteem and wanted students to like them above all else. Instead of developing healthy relationships with their peers, they seemed stuck in their childhood or adolescence. Regardless of the motivation, inappropriate boundaries can be damaging and dangerous in any school community. Inappropriate behavior includes:

- Joking around and making fun of students.

- Not enforcing school-wide agreements, including but not limited to: allowing students into staff-only areas; allowing students not enrolled in their class to hang out in their classroom (when the student was supposed to be in another class); and marking students present when they are absent.
- Not sharing when a student is at risk of being harmed or hurting themselves because the adult doesn't want to betray their confidence.
- Talking about other teachers or staff members in a negative way, including making fun of other staff members.
- Having obvious favorite students who receive privileges, including special attention from the staff member. This attention does not need to be romantic for it to be inappropriate.

This type of staff behavior can be harmful, even in a restorative culture.

SUGGESTIONS FOR RESPONDING

This is another difficult issue to address. The best way forward is to have a direct conversation with the teacher or staff member. These conversations can be difficult to plan for but are a phenomenal opportunity for our own growth and the growth in any relationship. Many times, staff members have come to me with hurt or anger toward a colleague. I encourage them to go to the source, just as we ask our students and parents to do when they have a concern with a staff member, but not without some planning and coaching support. This type of conversation is not limited to dealing with this particular challenge. I've had this conversation with colleagues, friends, and my loved ones. One practice that helps is an annual letter to your staff, from you, that directly states your expectations that they have these conversations, with your support available. I've added an example of an open letter in the resources section at the end of the book, as I think it's an effective way to address this particular challenge.

HOW TO PREPARE FOR
DIFFICULT CONVERSATIONS

Difficult conversations are scary! We need to have these conversations if we really want to focus on creating strong communities. Being prepared and centering the goal of having the conversation helps to ease fear and fuels courage.

There are four steps to having a difficult conversation. The first step is to set a date and time to meet. The second step is to plan the conversation. Actually having the conversation is the third step, but that's not the end of the process. In the fourth step, you should share about how the conversation went and identify what went well and what you will do differently next time.

SET A TIME. Let the person that you need to talk to know that you need to talk. There is no wrong way to set up the meeting. I recommend keeping things general. It's always best to beat curiosity and share what you want to discuss in a general way. Because the person might want more details than you're ready to give, it's easiest to send an email or text.

It's best to have these meetings in person. If that's not possible, set up a video conference. It's important that participants are able to see each other's faces because it is the most respectful way to communicate during a difficult conversation.

If the conversation is with a loved one or peer, but not potentially part of an evaluative conversation, then the following example will work: "Hi. I'm hoping that we can set up a time to talk about (insert topic in general). Are you able to meet in person or virtually on either of these dates?"

If the conversation is with an employee and may be evaluative, the invitation should be sent via email: "Hello. I'd like to set up a time to talk about (insert topic in general). Please let me know if either of these dates work for you, if not, please send me an alternate date and time. Thank you!"

PLAN. Your planning will determine how you enter the conversation. When you sit down to plan, consider this perspective: you are going to approach this conversation with respect and love for yourself, the other person, the community, and the relationship. By preparing for this conversation, you are ensuring that you will maintain dignity for all involved.

I recommend writing down what you want to say in either narrative or note form. If you have a trusted friend or colleague, ask them for input and feedback on your plan.

There are four parts of the conversation: 1) the introduction; 2) statement of concern and clarity regarding expectations; 3) providing a space to listen, 4) identifying next steps for follow up and close.

INTRODUCTION. The best way to start a difficult conversation is with authentic positivity. When you are angry, annoyed, frustrated, in protective mode, or hurt, this can be a hard thing to do. Don't have the conversation until those emotions are calmed and you can authentically share.

Make sure to open the conversation by thanking the person for meeting with you. Then, share why this conversation is important and what you hope to gain from the conversation.

In the introduction, you should also tell the person why they are important to you. Why is this person an asset to your community? What do you genuinely appreciate about them? Why is your relationship with them important to you and to the greater school community/organization?

If you are nervous, scared, anxious, or worried about the conversation, it is absolutely okay to let the other person know that. Framing it in this way can help: "This is really uncomfortable for me, but our relationship and who you are in this school is so important to me that I'm willing to brave being nervous."

Decide with the other person if you want to use a talking piece for any part of this discussion. I recommend using it minimally while you first speak your thoughts and then using it for their response. After that you may fall into a very organic conversation. Or not. Use the tools needed to get through the conversation.

STATEMENT OF CONCERN AND CLARITY REGARDING EXPECTATIONS. It's now time to delve into the issue. Consider the following example of sharing about an incident that has prompted the conversation with clarity:

> I've noticed that your relationships with students are really important to you. Relationships are important to all of us, especially with people we've made it our career's purpose to teach.
>
> Two things have happened that I want to talk to you about. During my prep on Tuesday, I walked into the staff meeting room with another staff member to work on our intervention plan. There was a student talking on his phone. He told me that you gave him the key. When I asked if he was okay, he told me he was fine, he just needed to make a call to his cousin. I'm sharing this with you because we have agreed, as a staff, that we don't allow students in the staff lounge since we use that space for confidential and sensitive conversations.
>
> Maria, in ninth grade, confided in me that she's been really depressed and thinking about hurting herself. I reminded her that I'm a mandated reporter, and if she's being hurt or thinking of hurting herself, it's my responsibility to make sure she's safe. She became very upset and told me that it just helps her to talk to someone, and that she's spoken to you about this also, and you promised to keep it between you two since she said she was really going to hurt herself.
>
> I wanted to talk to you about these things because I know you really care about our students. I'm not your supervisor; I'm your colleague, and our work here is

important. We have agreed to embrace and act in a restorative way. And we have to do this in a way that maintains the expectations and agreements we have as a staff and in our profession.

PROVIDE SPACE TO LISTEN. Thank the person you are with for listening to you and offer them the space to share using the active listening techniques from the chapter by Dr. Enjolie Lafaurie and a statement like the following:

> Thank you so much for being so willing to talk to me. As I mentioned, this is difficult, but because you're important to me and our work, I'm willing to have this conversation. Again, my hope is that we will leave this time together with more clarity and a path forward. I'd like to offer you the space now to respond to what I've shared.

If the person you are speaking with becomes defensive, the planning you have put in place will help you remain grounded in your message.

IDENTIFY NEXT STEPS FOR FOLLOW UP AND CLOSE. Once they have shared, restate what you heard and work together toward next steps. Summarize the conversation and any agreements. Thank them for being so open and willing to listen and respond. Reinforce that being and working in this way really provides a frame for a healthy community:

> Thank you again for this time. It seems that we agree that we are committed to our community. Here is how we are going to move forward [state agreements]. We have also both expressed that we want to set up a regular time to meet and open this safe space for us to brave and address any potential issues.

REFLECT. The final step of having a difficult conversation is reflecting. Either in writing or with a trusted friend or colleague, share how the conversation went. What worked really well? What do you want to make sure you continue to do the next time you have to have a difficult conversation? How could the conversation have been better? Lastly, celebrate yourself for being brave and facing the discomfort of having this conversation.

LACK OF SUPPORT FROM ADMINISTRATION AND/OR COLLEAGUES

The best thing for any school community is for everyone to embrace the restorative mindset, heartset, and practices. The best circumstances are when an organization's leadership embraces, models, and supports this work. Unfortunately, in some systems, this is won't be the case. The same is true in your personal life. I have developed a restorative mind, heart, and way of being. However, this is not the way of being for all the people in my life. At this point in time, my eldest daughters are not open to engaging in circles/círculos where we can discuss and heal incidents of harm. I can't make them adopt the practice, but what I can do is continue to model and respond to challenges in this way. If you are integrating this into your classroom, school, or life and are struggling with the idea that bosses, colleagues, or loved ones are unwilling to participate, please know that you are not alone. I'm right here with you.

What we can't do is give up. We do this work because it is the way we want to walk in this life. We can't change others, but we can invite them and share our successes, challenges, and joy in this work.

SUGGESTIONS FOR RESPONDING

Anytime you gather to meet, remind the group that you are a restorative practitioner and guide check-in and check-out circles/círculos before and after your time together.

Provide articles, resources, and research about restorative practices that you may have accumulated or that come your way. Track and collect data that show the benefits of being restorative for students and the system.

Invite leadership and colleagues into your space to participate in the restorative way of being through circles. Teach students to facilitate circles and have them invite leadership and colleagues to join them.

HIGHLIGHTS FROM THE CLASSROOM
BY PEDRO TERRAZAS

DESIRED OUTCOME

As outsiders looking in, many times we expect a solution or some sort of validating outcome that makes us feel better or gives us a sense of coming out ahead. I don't believe this feeling repairs the harm done or experienced by any victim. Restorative practices means taking full responsibility for our behaviors and actions by:

- Asking how our behavior affected others.
- Accepting that the behavior came from a choice that could have been made differently.
- Acknowledging harm and taking steps to repair it when possible.
- Reforming or making changes to avoid future harming behaviors from happening.

This component of the restorative practices process is important but can be difficult at the same time. It's important because it promotes accountability: everyone is responsible for their actions. The difficult part is taking responsibility for harming another person and taking the initiative to meet face to face to address the harm done. Many times, this process can be even more painful than the initial injury. This is a very important opportunity for growth. We need to come face to face with our choices and behaviors to understand how they affect other people, and we need to grow from our mistakes.

Restorative practices are intended to help students, staff, counselors, administrators, and community, making all stakeholders responsible. Only then can we take steps to repair harm. When this opportunity is present in the system, we can then say that we are a restorative community implementing a restorative culture, and we can begin to heal.

— CHAPTER NINE —

Leadership Matters

L eadership is one of life's greatest honors. We are given the beautiful responsibility to guide people, systems, and change. The most effective leaders strive to be good people. They live and work in their light and provide space for their employees and teams to do the same. They understand that positive, healthy, and nurturing work environments produce amazing results for their organization. Effective leaders embrace growth, vulnerability, and healing while ensuring the same is provided to employees. They also recognize that harm in life and work is inevitable, and they commit to restoring and growing from these incidences.

Transformation of our community begins with healing. Our students and staff carry not only their pain but also that of their ancestors and of our planet. Challenges such as substance abuse, mental illness, sexual abuse, physical abuse and violence, abandonment and neglect, intergenerational poverty, racism, and sexism must be acknowledged in order to be overcome. School leaders should commit to providing healing experiences for families, staff, community, and individual students through trauma-informed care and restorative practices.

In addition to restorative practices, schools should partner with local mental, medical, and behavioral health organizations to provide needed resources to students, staff, and families. By partnering with postsecondary institutions and community organizations, students will have hands-on access to cutting-edge, culturally responsive mental and behavioral health experts to support youth and family healing. School-, district-, county-, and state-level educational leaders should be guiding this work.

Schools and educational systems are representative of society as a whole. I know experienced teachers, staff, principals, and superintendents who create systems that allow them to continue to live in and share their pain. These systems still produce good and sometimes even great outcomes—although not consistently. These leaders and systems I describe are neither all bad nor all good; they represent the human condition.

It is my true belief that we as educators, and especially those in leadership, should strive to be better. And to be better, we must embrace our truth, especially when it's uncomfortable, challenging, and apt to offer us the opportunity to work on our issues. Yet more often than not, educators and leaders are unwilling to live and work this way.

So what are the characteristics of those who can effectively lead this work? A willingness to be vulnerable. If you haven't done so, please read and listen to Brené Brown regarding her research and work on vulnerability. When we make the decision to move away from the punitive discipline system that just doesn't work and embrace restorative practices, we are asking our staff and students to be honest with themselves and others about their emotions, experiences, and beliefs. It's hard to face and share experiences that have caused you pain.

How do we know that we are living and working in such a system? How do we know that our colleagues are somehow stuck in their pain? How do we know that we are stuck in our own? The first two questions are much easier to identify than the last. Let me describe what harmful leadership looks and acts like. These leaders are:

INTELLIGENT. They know how to speak the language and manage the relationships that got them the leadership position. They know how to speak the language of someone who is student centered and holds high expectations for staff. These leaders may be experts in pedagogy or the latest trends in education. But their actions say something different. They create harm by not providing space for their staff. They talk a great game with their bosses and maybe even staff, but ultimately their actions stem from self-interest and don't have true value.

NOT REFLECTIVE. While they may embrace professional development and be ready to delve into the latest educational trends that promote student success, they don't embrace growth for themselves as human beings. These leaders are unable and potentially unwilling to accept constructive feedback or feedback that exposes a "weakness." They don't want to be seen as wrong or not knowing the answer. When offered the opportunity to grow through reflection, this leader turns away.

DRIVEN BY EGO. The role of "educational leader" is very important to this type of person—as is being in charge and seen as the boss. They are the first to take credit for positive outcomes and the first to blame others—including students, parents, colleagues, the district, and the school board—when things go wrong.

MICROMANAGERS. These leaders need to have control, which comes from not wanting to be seen as not having all the answers. They don't fully trust others to do the work—which leads to students and staff not feeling valued.

Do these descriptors remind you of anyone you have known and worked with, or worked for? Do some of these descriptors apply to you? If the descriptions sound like someone you know or work with, it's time to have a conversation about these behaviors and the impact on students, staff, and the school culture. Circle/círculo discussions are a way to provide leaders with an opportunity for authentic reflection.

SEE THE RESOURCES CHAPTER FOR CIRCLE/CÍRCULO
PROMPTS FOR SCHOOL LEADERS

Here are some suggestions for leaders who are committed to creating a restorative system:

BE BRAVE, AUTHENTIC,
AND VULNERABLE.

MODEL CIRCLES/CÍRCULOS,
CHECK-INS, AND MEDIATIONS.

LEAD YOUR TEAM IN COMMITTING
TO HONORING EACH PERSON'S
INHERENT DIGNITY.

PROVIDE TRAINING AND
RESOURCES FOR STAFF AND
STUDENTS TO ENHANCE
THEIR PRACTICE.

ESTABLISH AND KEEP REGULAR
CHECK-IN TIME WITH
INDIVIDUALS AND TEAMS.

PROVIDE COACHING AND FEEDBACK
ON CIRCLES/CÍRCULOS, CHECK-INS,
AND MEDIATION.

ASK FOR FEEDBACK ON FACILITATION
OF CIRCLES/CÍRCULOS, CHECK-INS,
AND/OR MEDIATION.

PROVIDE CONSISTENT CIRCLE/
CÍRCULO TIME DURING STAFF
MEETINGS WITH PREPARED
QUESTIONS BASED
ON CURRENT ISSUES OR EVENTS.

ENSURE THAT STAFF AT ALL
LEVELS ARE ENGAGED IN
RESTORATIVE PRACTICES.

BE OPEN TO LEARNING FROM
ALL MEMBERS OF YOUR
SCHOOL COMMUNITY.

Resources

EXAMPLES OF BELIEF STATEMENTS

We believe that the key to success is founded in relationships.

We believe one's past does not define one's future.

We believe community and collaboration have the power to produce amazing results.

We believe everyone deserves a voice and choice in determining her/his/their future.

We believe we are strengthened through nurturing growth in self and others.

We believe we all make choices and are responsible for the consequences.

We believe the voices of our community must be elevated through leadership development, advocacy, and essential skill building.

We believe individuals with lived experience in the justice system are part of the solution and that their voices have value.

We believe that, by practicing and teaching ancestral knowledge, we heal the trauma of colonization that exists within ourselves, our families, our communities, and Mother Earth. This work honors and protects the next seven generations. Our elders have taught us that what we do today—our thoughts, prayers, actions, and work—should be to benefit the world seven generations in the future.

EXAMPLES OF ORGANIZATIONS' CORE VALUES

Equity	Learning
Social justice	Integrity
Innovation	Healthy living

VALUE STATEMENT EXAMPLE: POWER AGREEMENTS

At the charter school where I served as the director/principal from 2012 through 2015, we had what was known as POWER agreements. These agreements represented the values of the school. This acronym was something that the dean of students, Tommy Valentino Ramirez, led the students in creating years before my arrival. While the agreements were in place, they weren't implemented throughout or as part of the entire school culture. As part of a response from an accreditation visit, we were tasked with identifying school-wide learner outcomes (SLOs). Our staff chose to use the already-identified POWER agreements to flesh out our expectations for students. This work became, and remains to this day, the school's foundation for decisions and conversations with students and staff.

What started out as agreements that individual students committed to as members of our school became a founding document for academic, behavioral, and professional expectations for students and staff. The POWER agreements are as follows:

As a graduate, I will maximize my POWER: Potential, Ownership, Wisdom, Expectations, and Respect.

P OTENTIAL. I strive to meet my full potential and will show this by:

- Developing a plan for life after high school (college/career).
- Valuing myself, others, and community.
- Acquiring the English language skills necessary for success in academic and social settings.

OWNERSHIP. I take ownership of my actions, life, future, school, and community, and demonstrate this by:

- Developing an understanding of self, personal attributes, and connection to community.
- Setting goals regarding personal growth and community responsibility.
- Engaging in collective action that addresses community needs.

WISDOM. I use my wisdom to guide my words and actions to:

- Demonstrate an understanding that my actions and choices have a short- and long-term impact on others and our surroundings.
- Act as a critical thinker who transfers knowledge, makes connections, and applies learning across content areas and in life.

EXPECTATIONS. I have high expectations of myself and our community and express this by:

- Working independently and collaboratively to achieve success.
- Maintaining mentally, physically, and socially healthy behaviors.

RESPECT. I respect myself, others, our community, school, and environment by:

- Accepting and celebrating diversity.
- Understanding and utilizing restorative justice.
- Acting honestly, ethically, fairly, and empathetically.

These POWER agreements are an authentic example of what it means to truly live and breathe your organization's values and use them to establish tangible expectations for students.

MISSION STATEMENT EXAMPLE #1

This team, in partnership with community and internal stakeholders, will create and sustain an environment where our students are prepared for college, career, and lifetime self-sufficiency through academic, behavioral, and social supports integrated with real-world college, career, and community experiences.

MISSION STATEMENT EXAMPLE #2

We inspire leadership through community mentorship, resiliency building, advocacy, and system transformation for high-need individuals and families.

VISION STATEMENT EXAMPLE

All students and staff will be provided with:

- Multiple opportunities for voice and choice;
- Consistent recognition of achievement;
- Comprehensive and individualized support; and
- Engagement with, and as, alumnae of our system.

To ensure college and career readiness, our team will guarantee that:

- CTE courses are available;
- A comprehensive work-readiness program includes life skills and financial literacy;
- All students complete a digital college- and career-readiness portfolio;
- Locations exist throughout the county to provide career services and CTE instruction;
- All students are exposed to college and university opportunities; and
- Individualized support continues after graduation.

We will provide all students with exposure to career pathways that include:

- Academic, behavioral, and social support through input and active participation from partnerships with industry advisors and other stakeholders;
- A comprehensive, skills-based CTE curriculum aligned with industry standards;
- Work-based learning;
- Real-world internships and multiple career opportunities;
- Tiered skills development leading to industry-recognized certification; and
- Job placement assistance.

Exposure to career pathways may also include:

- Postsecondary support; and
- Community college dual enrollment.

PROMPTS FOR INTRODUCING STUDENT AND FAMILY GROUPS TO RESTORATIVE PRACTICES

Do you feel safe in our schools and classrooms? Why or why not?

How do you feel about our current disciplinary practices?

What parts of our disciplinary practices are working? What needs to be improved?

SAMPLE CHECK-OUT PROMPTS

What are one to three words that describe how you feel after our time together?

What are one to three things you are committed to doing after you leave today?

What is one thing that someone said or did today that surprised you?

What are one to three things that you learned from someone else today?

What is one thing you learned about yourself (or was reinforced)?

What is one thing you will take back to the classroom or your work?

What is one word that describes how you feel after our time together?

PROMPTS FOR YOUR CIRCLE/CÍRCULO

Below are some prompts for an introductory or new círculo:

Share a happy memory.

Do you like the mornings or evenings better and why?

Tell the story of your name.

If you could be a superhero, what superpowers would you choose and why?

How would your best friend/mom/teacher/boss describe you?

If you had an unexpected free day, what would you do?

If you were an animal, what would you be and why?

What are you looking forward to over the next break/holiday?

What's your favorite holiday and why?

Tell us about the best/worst teacher you've ever had (without saying their name).

Circles can also be used to discuss hot topics in your classroom, school, local community, or society. Pay attention to what is impacting your students and use a circle/círculo to provide an opportunity for reflection.

When creating prompts, make sure they are open-ended and require more than just a yes-or-no answer.

Have you been disrespected? How?

How do you feel about how we work as a class/team?

How have you been affected, hurt, or harmed by the way we work as a team?

What is a regret you have that you are willing to share?

SAMPLE SENTENCE STARTERS FOR FISHBOWLS

What are your hopes for the future?

What are your greatest challenges?

Tell us about your support system.

What does it mean to be a man/woman/transgender person in your family or culture?

How have you been elevated by the people in your life?

Share an experience you have had with someone who is of a different sexual orientation than you are.

What would someone on the outside group be surprised to know about you?

"I heard . . ."

"I learned . . ."

"I was surprised by . . ."

"I appreciated . . ."

SAMPLE QUESTIONS TO INITIATE MEDIATION

What are the facts of what happened?

What did you do?

How did that make you feel?

What were you thinking at the time?

What have you thought about since then?

Who has been affected by what you have done? In what way?

What do you think you need to do to make things right?

What impact did this incident have on you and others?

What has been the hardest thing for you?

SAMPLE AFFIRMATIONS

"From what you're describing to me, it sounds like . . ."

"I can understand why that would make you upset/angry/hurt/ feel disrespected. Is there anything that you did or said that contributed to what happened?"

SAMPLE STEP-FORWARD PROMPTS

You love chocolate chip cookies.

You were born in (name the city/state you're in).

You are an only child.

Your first language was not English.

You have more than four siblings.

You sleep really well every night.

You have been in love.

You or someone you love has been homeless.

You love playing video games.

You have had your heart broken.

You or someone you love has ever been to jail or prison.

You've ever ridden a horse.

You were raised in a home with both parents.

You were born in another country.

You have ever felt alone.

You have been impacted by domestic violence.

You have ever been hungry because you or your family didn't have enough food.

You can play a musical instrument.

You have ever considered suicide.

You know exactly what you want to do with your life after high school.

You're scared or worried about life after high school.

You have ever been so happy that your heart almost felt like it was bursting.

You could have stepped forward but didn't.

SAMPLE PROMPTS FOR ACTIVE OBSERVERS

What did you hear in the circle/círculo that resonated with you?

How did the circle/círculo evolve as more participants shared?

What do you appreciate about someone in the circle/círculo?

What did you notice about the process used to pass around the talking piece?

SAMPLE PROMPTS ABOUT VULNERABILITY

What can be difficult about the circle/círculo and sharing?

Share about a time you felt vulnerable.

Share about a time someone took advantage of your trust.

Share about a time you confided in someone. How did it feel?

How is vulnerability viewed in your family or culture?

Share about a time you saw someone do something that you consider brave.

Think about someone you admire for being courageous. Describe what they do that makes them brave.

SAMPLE PROMPTS FOR RESTORATIVE PRACTICES FACILITATION

What are the benefits of restorative practices?

How has engaging in circles/círculos impacted you as a person? As an educator or student? In your personal life?

Discuss successes you've had with students and parents.

Discuss the most challenging thing about facilitating circles.

CIRCLE/CÍRCULO PROMPTS FOR SCHOOL LEADERS

Who are you and why are you here? *This prompt gives you an opportunity to learn a lot about those that you're working with.*

Tell us why you've chosen to accept the responsibility of being an educational leader.

How do leaders exhibit authenticity or create authentic systems?

What are the fears leaders have that keep them from being vulnerable with their teams?

What role does self-awareness have in your growth as a leader?

Why is it important to create a space in the workplace for harm to be acknowledged and healed?

Describe the characteristics of great leaders.

MORE SAMPLE PROMPTS

How do restorative practices used in schools with students and staff benefit the school community?

What are the emotional benefits of creating space for students and staff to connect with one another?

What activities do you use to create a space for students and/or staff to connect with one another?

What are the academic or professional benefits of creating space for students and staff to connect with one another?

What are the barriers and challenges facing teachers and school leaders that keep them from creating space for student and staff connection?

How do you, or the school system in which you work, respond to students or staff resistant to participating in activities that promote connection?

Share about a time you worked in an organization that faced a challenge.

Tell us about a time that you faced change.

Tell us about a time you needed someone's help.

Tell a story about a holiday tradition you observe.

What makes someone a good friend?

Share about a time a friend really had your back or you had theirs.

Share about a time that a friend let you down.

Share about a time that you let a friend down.

Share about a time that a parent or family member let you down.

Share about a time that you let a parent or family member down.

Tell us about a time that you got away with something.

Tell us about a time that you got caught doing something you knew was wrong.

How has the school system harmed your students?

How does the school system perpetuate harm for students and staff?

Why is healing important and in what ways have you experienced healing?

Please share about a time that you were harmed by someone in the school system.

- What did you think and feel when you realized what had happened?
- What systems were in place to support you after being harmed?
- Have you healed or grown from this experience? If so, how? If not, what are the barriers to preventing healing or growth?
- How has this experience helped you to support those who've been harmed and to prevent you from harming others?

AN OPEN LETTER TO OUR SCHOOL STAFF

The following letter is a model of one that I would frequently write, review, and provide to my staff at the start of every school year. My first principal, Karen Janney, provided staff with a letter just like this. I then used my version for years before I had even heard of restorative practices or restorative justice. While this letter doesn't mention restorative practices, as you read through it, you will find many elements of the practices. It serves as a sample of what a teacher, manager, or principal can share with their team while providing clarity on expectations for all.

I have put these notes and thoughts together for all the teachers and staff at our school in the spirit of setting clear expectations. We are each to be considered a "teacher," and I will use this term, in this document, to identify all staff at our school. Should our expectations not fit your philosophy, we can all avoid disappointment by being clear and honest with one another.

We have established an innovative educational system guaranteeing four fundamental experiences: healing, problem-based learning, career readiness, and youth/parent leadership development. Our school exists to meet the comprehensive needs of students and families in our community. Our goal is to support students and families in overcoming barriers they may experience such as: poverty, language, substance abuse, domestic violence, teen pregnancy, gang involvement, crime, and homelessness.

At our school we expect our students to embrace, explore, and act using their POWER (potential, ownership, wisdom, expectations, and respect). We expect the same from the staff.

Purpose: We are each charged with motivating our students to become social agents of positive change for our community while providing a rigorous learning experience. We do this through problem-based learning, using content standards to ensure college and career readiness while exploring our world through the lens of social justice. Regardless of your position at our school, you are charged with the goal of supporting students in earning their high school diploma, helping them plan for college/career, and motivating them to become social agents of positive change for our community.

Role Models: I expect you to be an example of compassion, self-control, consideration, work habits, language, and dress. Expect students to be prompt with their work and submit requested work in a timely manner. Expect students to be on time and ensure you arrive to work by 8:00 a.m. every day. Expect students to solve conflict using their POWER. You should do the same. In the classroom, you must be well prepared with your lesson, well organized, and have audiovisual or written materials ready. In the office and during meetings, arrive prepared and ready to work and learn.

Teacher/Student Relationships: At our school we have students from extremely diverse backgrounds and those who have championed through life overcoming many challenges. From experience, I have learned that every successful relationship is based on trust and respect. It is my hope to hire and maintain teachers who truly care about our students and their success in life. Teachers must successfully manage trusting and respectful relationships with students without trying to overcompensate for what students lack. They don't need a savior; they need a teacher who cares enough to show up every day, ready to provide a rich and challenging learning experience that they are guaranteed to succeed in, and they need a teacher who consistently enforces our common expectations, policies, and procedures. Our students need you to provide each of them with the best of you, so it is important to be aware of actions that may create favoritism.

Relationships with Colleagues: The staff at our school is a family, bound by our commitment to provide our students with the most meaningful learning experience possible. We realize that some of our students enter our classrooms with the experience of failure, and we are driven to lead them to embrace the possibilities of a bright future through a quality education. We must stand united in this adventure. Communication with each other is crucial to our success as staff. In order to create a united and supportive front, we must consistently enforce and practice our school policies, procedures, and agreements. If a student seeks you out to complain about a situation with another teacher, it's important that you don't appear to take sides but manage the conversation to support that student in respectfully resolving their concerns. Just as I do, always assume best intentions first.

Handling Conflict: If you are having an issue with any member of our school community (student, parent, or colleague), I am here to listen and help you plan how to share the issue in a respectful way, but I will not have the conversation for you. You are responsible for your relationships with all members of our community and must face the uncomfortable feeling of conflict in a manner that is respectful to both parties. If you need support in planning for these challenging conversations, I am here for you.

Discipline/Classroom Management: Discipline is the responsibility of all persons at our school. It is our role to celebrate and reinforce positive choices as well as to address inappropriate behavior through restorative justice. I expect everyone to be aware of student conduct and to immediately address inappropriate behavior, language, and attitude through respectful dialogue. Discipline and teaching are the responsibilities of all school staff. Staff will not ignore behavior that is counter to our POWER agreements. All teachers are expected to handle improper student behavior in a calm, firm, and fair way.

Classroom teachers enter the room with the charge of teaching students content-area standards through project-based learning using critical pedagogy. This is a heady combination that is only possible through the creation and maintenance of a safe, positive, and compassionate learning environment. Students need you to be in control of the classroom while respecting and allowing student voice. You need to be very clear with yourself and them about classroom expectations. It is important to start every class period ready to greet students at the door. In order to prevent undesired behavior, you are responsible for planning activities that engage them. If students are kept active, they will be far less likely to act out.

Parent/Family Contact: Although our students may be older, it is still your responsibility to make personal contact with parents or family representatives regarding their progress. Contact can happen via phone, email, conferences, or home visits. It is always best to have positive communication with students' families as close to the start of the session as possible. Family contact must be made prior to asking for intervention from an administrator.

Administrative Support: I am here for you and will always support you in doing what is in the best interest of our students. Do not expect that because you are a teacher, I will say you are right if you make a poor choice. I will help you handle the problem and help you work on a win-win situation to calm the conflict. I will never speak negatively of you to students or parents. However, I will expect you to think before you act or speak, and I ask you not to create situations where if pressed with the question, "Was the teacher correct in taking that action or speaking in that manner?" I must answer, "No."

Our time together as a staff is limited and must be focused on our collective work. Any announcement or daily, business-type information must be sent out via email. You are expected to check your school email twice a day (before first period and sometime after lunch). This will help keep you in the loop. You will receive a weekly FYI that will provide reminders and important information. Expect to see me in your classroom on a regular basis. I will make every effort to leave a note for you around your desk area. Communication is key to our success.

Grades and Teacher Class Policy: You will be expected to submit your curriculum map and class syllabus with a grading policy to me at the beginning of each session. We have three grading periods every session, but I encourage you to provide assessment information to students and parents on a regular basis. When asked to meet with a student regarding progress, I will ask for a current grading sheet.

Our Way: Our school is a caring and supportive environment where students can learn and grow as individuals. I want us to be known as a school where students and staff strive for academic and personal excellence and where everyone is included in the plan to get there. This attitude and behavior start with us. If our way is a philosophy that you can support, nurture, and demand, then I welcome you to our community.

—Marisol Rerucha, Principal

Glossary

Abuelita: Grandmother.

Active listening: Listening to others with dignity, respect, and your heart and mind.

Active observing: The act of constantly being aware of what others are communicating about their emotional state in both verbal and nonverbal ways.

Agreements: A guideline or process for healing that gives voice to the individuals involved in a conflict that has occurred. The agreements are set forth to prevent future conflicts and to support the social-emotional growth of the gente involved.

Ancestors: Those who lived before or during our time but who have now passed to the afterlife. We pray to our ancestors in gratitude, for protection, and for guidance.

Carga: An emotional burden or pain a person has been carrying that has been keeping them from growing or being successful.

Check-in/Check-out: A way to connect with one another at the start and end of meetings.

Chicana/o: Term of pride used by Mexican-American activists. This term was coined in the 1960s during the Civil Rights Movement.

Circle/Círculo: A group of individuals, led by a facilitator, who engage in reflection and discussion regarding issues happening in the community. The circles can take many forms.

Desmadroso: A person who engages in unruly behavior that can lead to other disruptive actions.

Elders: Our relatives who are older than us and who share knowledge, stories, and a history of our people and families.

Forgiveness: An intentional decision that releases any negative energy or feelings from a person or group of people that have done harm to another person.

Gente: The people or group you share an identity with.

Harm: An incident or experience that has imposed any negative energy from one person on another. The energy can come in physical or emotional form.

Indígena/Indigenous: Our people who are native to the land and who practice traditional ways of being connected to one another, the earth, and all elements.

Mediation: An intensive circle, facilitated by a trusted community member, focused on an issue between two or more community members.

Palabra: "Word" in English. It's an agreement made between two or more people. When you give your palabra you are giving your word, speaking your truth, making a promise or commitment.

Relatives: We are connected by our humanity and are all relatives regardless of shared blood. Each time we greet each other, reach out to help, or ask for help from one another, we are honoring our relation.

Sagrado: Sacred. Something to be regarded with great and utmost respect and honor.

Talking piece: An item that is used during circles or dialogue that is passed around from speaker to speaker. Only those with the talking piece should be speaking.

Temazcal: A type of sweat lodge used for community prayer and healing in Latin American countries for centuries.

Trauma: The way one's emotional and physical state is compromised by a negative experience.

References

Berven, Norman L., Kenneth R. Thomas, and Fong Chan. 2004. "An Introduction to Counseling for Rehabilitation Health Professionals," in *Counseling Theories and Techniques for Rehabilitation Health Professionals*, edited by Fong Chan, Norman L. Berven, and Kenneth. R. Thomas. New York: Springer.

Bilston, Brian, and José Sanabria. 2019. *Refugees*. London: Palazzo Editions.

Bohart, Arthur C., and Karen Tallman. 1999. *How Clients Make Therapy Work: The Process of Active Self-Healing*. Washington, DC: American Psychological Association.

Boyle, Greg. 2016. "Connecting Through Kinship." Keynote address at Global Homeboy Network, California Endowment, Los Angeles, CA.

Bozarth, Jerold D., Fred M. Zimring, and Reinhard Tausch. 2002. "Client-Centered Therapy: The Evolution of a Revolution." In *Humanistic Psychotherapies: Handbook of Research and Practice*, edited by David J. Cain and Julius Seeman, 147–88. Washington, DC: American Psychological Association.

Brown, Brené. 2017. *Rising Strong: How the Ability to Reset Transforms the Way We Live, Love, Parent, and Lead*. New York: Random House.

Chan, Fong, Norman L. Berven, and Kenneth R. Thomas. 2004. *Counseling Theories and Techniques for Rehabilitation and Mental Health Professionals*. New York: Springer Publishing Company.

Circles for Change. 2017. "Introduction to Council Training Materials."

Corey, Gerald. 2015. *Theory and Practice of Counseling and Psychotherapy*. Boston: Cengage Learning.

Covey, Stephen R. 1989. *The Seven Habits of Highly Effective People.* New York: Simon and Schuster.

Cramer, Sharon F. 1998. *Collaboration: A Success Strategy for Special Educators.* Boston: Allyn and Bacon.

Felitti, Vincent J., Robert F. Anda, Dale Nordenberg, David F. Williamson, Alison M. Spitz, Valerie Edwards, Mary P. Koss, and James S. Marks. 1998. "Relationship of Childhood Abuse and Household Dysfunction to Many of the Leading Causes of Death in Adults: The Adverse Childhood Experiences (ACE) Study." *American Journal of Preventive Medicine* 14, no. 4: 245.

Gordon, Thomas. 1975. *P.E.T.: Parent Effectiveness Training: The Tested New Way to Raise Responsible Children.* New York: New American Library.

Gregory, Anne, and Katherine R. Evans. 2020. "The Starts and Stumbles of Restorative Justice in Education: Where Do We Go from Here?" National Education Policy Center. https://nepc .colorado.edu/publication/restorative-justice.

Hicks, Donna. 2011. *Dignity.* New Haven and London: Yale University Press.

Hooker, David Anderson, and Amy Potter Czajkowski. 2012. *Transforming Historical Harms.* Harrisonburg, VA: Eastern Mennonite University.

Levitt, Dana Heller. 2002. "Active Listening and Counselor Self-Efficacy: Emphasis on One Microskill in Beginning Counselor Training." *Clinical Supervisor* 20, no. 2: 101–115.

Mansfield, Kathryn. 2017. "Strategies for Trauma Awareness and Resilience Programme: Experiential Education Towards Resilience and Trauma Informed People and Practice." *Intervention* 15, no. 3: 264–277.

McNaughton, David, Dawn Hamlin, John McCarthy, Darlene Head-Reeves, and Mary Schreiner. 2008. "Learning to Listen: Teaching an Active Listening Strategy to Preservice Education

Professionals." *Topics in Early Childhood Special Education* 27, no. 4: 223–31.

Medley, Grace, Rachel N. Lipari, Jonaki Bose, Devon S. Cribb, Larry A. Kroutil, and Gretchen McHenry. 2016. "Sexual Orientation and Estimates of Adult Substance Use and Mental Health: Results from the 2015 National Survey on Drug Use and Health." Washington, DC: Substance Abuse and Mental Health Services Administration.

Miller-Karas, Elaine. 2015. *Building Resilience to Trauma: The Trauma and Community Resiliency Models.* New York: Routledge.

O'Shea, Dorothy, Lawrence O'Shea, Robert Algozzine, Diana J. Hammittee. 2000. *Families and Teachers of Individuals with Disabilities: Collaborative Orientations and Responsive Practices.* Boston: Allyn & Bacon.

Orlov, A. B. 1992. "Carl Rogers and Contemporary Humanism." *Journal of Russian and East European Psychology* 30, no. 1: 36–41.

Pearce, C. Glenn, Iris W. Johnson, and Randolph T. Barker. 2003. "Assessment of the Listening Styles Inventory: Progress in Establishing Reliability and Validity." *Journal of Business and Technical Communication* 17, no. 1: 84–113.

Riel, Margaret, and Kathleen Fulton. 2001. "The Role of Technology in Supporting Learning Communities." *Phi Delta Kappan* 82, no. 7: 518–523.

Rogers, Carl R. 1951. *Client-Centered Therapy: Its Current Practice, Implications, and Theory.* Boston: Houghton-Mifflin.

Spataro, Susan E., and Janel Bloch. 2018. "'Can You Repeat That?' Teaching Active Listening in Management Education." *Journal of Management Education* 42, no. 2: 168–98.

Tschannen-Moran, Megan, and Wayne Hoy. 1997. "Trust in Schools: A Conceptual and Empirical Analysis." *Journal of Educational Administration* 36, no. 4: 334–352.

Turnbull, Ann P., and H. Rutherford Turnbull. 1990. *Families, Professionals, and Exceptionality: A Special Partnership*. 2nd ed. New York: Merrill.

Van der Kolk, Bessel. 2014. *The Body Keeps the Score: Brain, Mind, and Body in the Healing of Trauma*. New York: Penguin.

Vander Ark, T. 2004. "Leading Small Secondary School Learning Communities." Paper presented at the NCTAF Summit Two: Transforming schools into strong learning communities, Wingspread Conference Center, Racine, WI.

Vanzant, Iyanla. 2012. "Why You Should Put Yourself First." *Oprah's Lifeclass: The Tour*, Oprah Winfrey Network, 28 March 2012. https://www.youtube.com/watch?v=ZhqokZF5OFU&feature=youtu.be.

Weger, Harry, Jr., Gina Castle Bell, Elizabeth M. Minei, and Melissa C. Robinson. 2010. "The Relative Effectiveness of Active Listening in Initial Interactions." *International Journal of Listening* 28, no. 1: 13–31.

Weger, Harry, Jr., Gina R. Castle, and Melissa C. Emmett. 2010. "Active Listening in Peer Interviews: The Influence of Message Paraphrasing on Perceptions of Listening Skill." *International Journal of Listening* 24, no. 1: 34–49.

Wenger, Etienne. 1998. *Communities of Practice: Learning, Meaning and Identity*. Cambridge: Cambridge University Press.

Wenger, Ettiene. 1998. "Communities of Practice: Learning as a Social System." *Systems Thinker* 9, no. 5: 2–3.

Yellow Horse Brave Heart, Maria. 2003. "The Historical Trauma Response Among Natives and Its Relationship with Substance Abuse: A Lakota Illustration." *Journal of Psychoactive Drugs* 35, no. 1: 7–13.

Zehr, Howard. 2008 "Doing Justice, Healing Trauma: The Role of Restorative Justice in Peacebuilding." *South Asian Journal of Peacebuilding* 1, no. 1: 1–16.

About the Author

MARISOL QUEVEDO RERUCHA is a proven leader who doesn't just talk about healing, equity, social justice, and disrupting generational trauma; she has both lived experience and a proven record of doing this work while leading change in education and nonprofit systems. As a Chicana, mother, former teacher, principal, district leader, and nonprofit leader, she uses her voice to challenge systems of oppression and—more importantly—amplifies the voices of others. The impact of her passion, experience, work, and voice is felt beyond her own community as she serves as chief of strategy and partnerships for the National Parents Union; director of culture and community for Dave Burgess Consulting, Inc.; chair of the UnidosUS National Institute for Latino School Leaders alumni council; board member of Youth Empowerments Finest; and a partner with organizations (nonprofit and for-profit businesses) to provide comprehensive strategic-action planning and restorative practices.

More From

Dave Burgess Consulting, Inc.

Since 2012, DBCI has published books that inspire and equip educators to be their best. For more information on our titles or to purchase bulk orders for your school, district, or book study, visit DaveBurgessConsulting.com/DBCIbooks.

More from the *Like a PIRATE*™ Series

Teach Like a PIRATE by Dave Burgess

eXPlore Like a PIRATE by Michael Matera

Learn Like a PIRATE by Paul Solarz

Play Like a PIRATE by Quinn Rollins

Run Like a PIRATE by Adam Welcome

Tech Like a PIRATE by Matt Miller

Lead *Like a PIRATE*™ Series

Lead Like a PIRATE by Shelley Burgess and Beth Houf

Balance Like a PIRATE by Jessica Cabeen, Jessica Johnson, and Sarah Johnson

Lead beyond Your Title by Nili Bartley

Lead with Appreciation by Amber Teamann and Melinda Miller

Lead with Culture by Jay Billy

Lead with Instructional Rounds by Vicki Wilson

Lead with Literacy by Mandy Ellis

Leadership & School Culture

Culturize by Jimmy Casas

Escaping the School Leader's Dunk Tank by Rebecca Coda and Rick Jetter

Fight Song by Kim Bearden

From Teacher to Leader by Starr Sackstein

If the Dance Floor Is Empty, Change the Song by Joe Clark

The Innovator's Mindset by George Couros

It's OK to Say "They" by Christy Whittlesey

Kids Deserve It! by Todd Nesloney and Adam Welcome

Let Them Speak by Rebecca Coda and Rick Jetter

The Limitless School by Abe Hege and Adam Dovico

Live Your Excellence by Jimmy Casas

Next-Level Teaching by Jonathan Alsheimer

The Pepper Effect by Sean Gaillard

Principaled by Kate Barker, Kourtney Ferrua, and Rachael George

The Principled Principal by Jeffrey Zoul and Anthony McConnell

Relentless by Hamish Brewer

The Secret Solution by Todd Whitaker, Sam Miller, and Ryan Donlan

Start. Right. Now. by Todd Whitaker, Jeffrey Zoul, and Jimmy Casas

Stop. Right. Now. by Jimmy Casas and Jeffrey Zoul

Teachers Deserve It by Rae Hughart and Adam Welcome

Teach Your Class Off by CJ Reynolds

They Call Me "Mr. De" by Frank DeAngelis

Thrive through the Five by Jill M. Siler

Unmapped Potential by Julie Hasson and Missy Lennard

When Kids Lead by Todd Nesloney and Adam Dovico

Word Shift by Joy Kirr

Your School Rocks by Ryan McLane and Eric Lowe

Technology & Tools

50 Things You Can Do with Google Classroom by Alice Keeler and Libbi Miller

50 Things to Go Further with Google Classroom by Alice Keeler and Libbi Miller

140 Twitter Tips for Educators by Brad Currie, Billy Krakower, and Scott Rocco

Block Breaker by Brian Aspinall

Building Blocks for Tiny Techies by Jamila "Mia" Leonard

Code Breaker by Brian Aspinall

The Complete EdTech Coach by Katherine Goyette and Adam Juarez

Control Alt Achieve by Eric Curts

The Esports Education Playbook by Chris Aviles, Steve Isaacs, Christine Lion-Bailey, and Jesse Lubinsky

Google Apps for Littles by Christine Pinto and Alice Keeler

Master the Media by Julie Smith

Reality Bytes by Christine Lion-Bailey, Jesse Lubinsky, and Micah Shippee, PhD

Sail the 7 Cs with Microsoft Education by Becky Keene and Kathi Kersznowski

Shake Up Learning by Kasey Bell

Social LEADia by Jennifer Casa-Todd

Stepping Up to Google Classroom by Alice Keeler and Kimberly Mattina

Teaching Math with Google Apps by Alice Keeler and Diana Herrington

Teachingland by Amanda Fox and Mary Ellen Weeks

Teaching Methods & Materials

All 4s and 5s by Andrew Sharos

Boredom Busters by Katie Powell

The Classroom Chef by John Stevens and Matt Vaudrey

The Collaborative Classroom by Trevor Muir

Copyrighteous by Diana Gill

CREATE by Bethany J. Petty

Ditch That Homework by Matt Miller and Alice Keeler

Ditch That Textbook by Matt Miller

Don't Ditch That Tech by Matt Miller, Nate Ridgway, and Angelia Ridgway

EDrenaline Rush by John Meehan

Educated by Design by Michael Cohen, The Tech Rabbi

The EduProtocol Field Guide by Marlena Hebern and Jon Corippo

The EduProtocol Field Guide: Book 2 by Marlena Hebern and Jon Corippo

Game On? Brain On! by Lindsay Portnoy, PhD

Innovating Play by Jessica LaBar-Twomy and Christine Pinto

Instant Relevance by Denis Sheeran

LAUNCH by John Spencer and A.J. Juliani

Make Learning MAGICAL by Tisha Richmond

Pass the Baton by Kathryn Finch and Theresa Hoover

Project-Based Learning Anywhere by Lori Elliott

Pure Genius by Don Wettrick

The Revolution by Darren Ellwein and Derek McCoy

Shift This! by Joy Kirr

Skyrocket Your Teacher Coaching by Michael Cary Sonbert

Spark Learning by Ramsey Musallam

Sparks in the Dark by Travis Crowder and Todd Nesloney

Table Talk Math by John Stevens

Unpack Your Impact by Naomi O'Brien and LaNesha Tabb

The Wild Card by Hope and Wade King

The Writing on the Classroom Wall by Steve Wyborney

Inspiration, Professional Growth & Personal Development

Be REAL by Tara Martin

Be the One for Kids by Ryan Sheehy

The Coach ADVenture by Amy Illingworth

Creatively Productive by Lisa Johnson

Educational Eye Exam by Alicia Ray

The EduNinja Mindset by Jennifer Burdis

Empower Our Girls by Lynmara Colón and Adam Welcome

Finding Lifelines by Andrew Grieve and Andrew Sharos

The Four O'Clock Faculty by Rich Czyz

How Much Water Do We Have? by Pete and Kris Nunweiler

P Is for Pirate by Dave and Shelley Burgess

A Passion for Kindness by Tamara Letter

The Path to Serendipity by Allyson Apsey

Sanctuaries by Dan Tricarico

Saving Sycamore by Molly B. Hudgens

The SECRET SAUCE by Rich Czyz

Shattering the Perfect Teacher Myth by Aaron Hogan

Stories from Webb by Todd Nesloney

Talk to Me by Kim Bearden

Teach Better by Chad Ostrowski, Tiffany Ott, Rae Hughart, and Jeff Gargas

Teach Me, Teacher by Jacob Chastain

Teach, Play, Learn! by Adam Peterson

The Teachers of Oz by Herbie Raad and Nathan Lang-Raad

TeamMakers by Laura Robb and Evan Robb

Through the Lens of Serendipity by Allyson Apsey

The Zen Teacher by Dan Tricarico

Children's Books

Beyond Us by Aaron Polansky

Cannonball In by Tara Martin

Dolphins in Trees by Aaron Polansky

I Want to Be a Lot by Ashley Savage

The Princes of Serendip by Allyson Apsey

Ride with Emilio by Richard Nares

The Wild Card Kids by Hope and Wade King

Zom-Be a Design Thinker by Amanda Fox